True Confessions

and

New Clichés

All the very best

for Gullhead. 93

LIZ · LOCHHEAD
TRUE
CONFESSIONS
& · NEW · CLICHES

POLYGON · BOOKS

© Liz Lochhead 1985
Polygon
22 George Square, Edinburgh

First published in 1985
Revised and reprinted 1986
Reprinted 1989
Reprinted 1993

Typeset by Polyprint, Edinburgh
and printed in Great Britain by
Redwood Press Ltd, Melksham, Wiltshire

ISBN 0 7486 6156 5

The publisher acknowledges subsidy from the
Scottish Arts Council towards the publication of
this volume.

For my Mum, Margaret,
and all the Merryhellers.

Contents

Contents

Sugar and Spite
and
True Confessions

Sugar and Spite was the first attempt at doing anything specifically for out-loud performance. In spring 1978, Marcella Evaristi had persuaded the Traverse that she and I ought to put a "poetry reading" together, and run it for several nights. "What, the same poems, every night the same order, *planning* it?" "Yes, and wouldn't it be good to get a structure and ... maybe costume, a few props anyway and *learn* the poems off by heart, not read them, nose buried in a book, dropping them out your looseleaf onto the floor,scrabbling around picking them up again in the wrong order." "You mean a sort of *show* ..." "Why not."

But not many poems felt at all right to do out loud. Only "Spinster"* and "Bawd",* two poems that I suddenly realised were dramatic monologues anyway. So Marcella and I started writing loads more. ... And it seemed there ought to be music, so Esther Allan, the music teacher at the school where I was the most reluctant member of the Art Department, got roped in. As neither Marcella or I could sing we spoke along to the music in what we felt, somehow, was Good Old Cabaret Style ... Esther sang the songs that were proper songs. It was great fun to do and people seemed to like it, so I was hooked. More of this.

True Confessions in 1981 was an attempt at getting my stage nerve back after a disastrous premature version of *Blood and Ice*, my first try at a real play, went on in the studio of the Belgrade Theatre, Coventry ("I'd rather be at the dentist — Birmingham Evening News"). So would I, and the cast too. I kept trying to remember what a good time *Sugar and Spite* had been — and *Goodstyle*, a history of art revue I'd written and pinched and compiled for Duncan of Jordanstone College of Art, Dundee, when I'd been writer in residence. Maybe I ought to stick to revue?

One "character", Sharon, the schoolgirl who loves (among other things) the Brontes, had been written for *Sugar and Spite* and she didn't depend on rhyme for her humour and seemed less steam-radio-Stanley-Holloway-meets-Flanders-

1

and-Swann-meets-Joyce-Grenfell-old-fashioned. (I *liked* the radio when I was wee.) I thought I'd like to write more characters who, by being deadly serious, would give themselves away . . .

Siobhan Redmond I'd seen once in a revue by Marcella for St Andrews University and I tracked her down in Glasgow and asked her would she like to do a show for buttons for the newly opened Tron Theatre, who were interested. She said yes. Esther Allan dusted off the music and taught her the best songs from *Sugar and Spite*. We both thought Siobhan was brilliant. This inspired me to write the dreadful Verena for her. (Siobhan provided the "basically" Verena threaded things together with.) "Suzanne Valadon" was rescued from the *Goodstyle* script and its patchy Franglais with Frenchy music by Esther was something Siobhan made all her own. Some things were revived and rewritten from *Sugar and Spite* but Esther and I both wrote like maniacs, together, separately, new stuff.

We got full houses (it was only the bar seating 65) and got asked back. Revived it at the Edinburgh Festival the following year with Angie Rew replacing Esther Allan who had fallen in love with a Frenchman and gone. We do bits together whenever we get the chance and (someday) will do a brand new one.

We spilt a few beans and touched the odd (female) nerve and laughed off a few fiascos. It seemed odd that taking the (gentle) mickey out of women (i.e. ourselves) made *some* men (not *our* Real Pals) feel a bit-got at. . . .

The subject was Women In Love. Hence *True Confessions*.

True Confessions
(Rap)

Wanna know anything 'bout being a woman?
Well, better just ask us.
I know her dramas, her traumas, and her fiascos
I know her sober
(but I know her better pissed)
I know her acid trips,
her abortions, and her analyst.
I know the Story of her Life —
each ironic twist.

She lent me her copy of Anais Nin
and we discovered we were Sisters Under the Skin.
Oh, I know her inside out —
thanks to the sessions
of all-and-sundry, dirty-laundry
True Confessions.

Our conversations range from the Arts to Child Psychology.
From World Affairs and Who Cares
To Avant-Garde Gynaecology.
I know her trouble with her nerves
and the trouble with her mate,
what she did with her brother when they were eight,
and Should-she-love-him? Should-she-leave-him?
What-were-their-Chances?
The night she was almost tempted by lesbian advances.
I know about the strange stains she found
on young Sebastian's pyjamas,
her Wild Night with that waiter
on her trip to the Bahamas;
I get the dope on each High Hope,
on her fainting spasms,
the ins-and-outs of her orgasms,
how the Pill gives her Headaches,
her cramps with the coil,
how My-Man-once-made-this-pass-at-her-at-a-party-but
She Was Too Loyal.

3

Oh, we spill the beans and we swill our gin
and discover that we're Sisters Under The Skin.
Oh, I know her inside out —
thanks to the sessions
of truly hellish, unembellished
True Confessions.

Open with the Closing
(Song)

You should never try to make a Lover
Of someone who ought to be a Friend
So let's open with the closing —
Begin with the end.

Don't have to be a Guggenheim scholar
To realise when I'm beat —
Don't get all hot under the collar
When I tell you I've got cold feet.

What right had I to think it might be easy?
Why was I so sure it should be fun?
You know we'd hate to complicate it—
So let's end it before it's begun.

First the phonecall, starter's orders
For an over-eager heart —
I was off before the pistol.
False start.

No, no, never try and make a lover
Of someone who ought to be a friend.
So let's open with the closing,
Begin with the end.

Mrs Abernethy: Burns the Hero
(Monologue)

Don't you think it would of been absolutely Super to have been Immortalised by Robert Burns? What a man, eh? I just have to agree with my Better Half on this one — he loves Poetry you know — why, his whole study in the Manse is absolutely chockabloc-jampacked with Poetry Books. Of course it's Yours Truly that's got to dust the whole kit and caboodle! Well, he likes, instead of sticking to Paul and the Ephesians all the time, to, you know, slip in a wee snippet of Shakespeare or Tennyson or mibbe even Wordsworth now and again, as a Text. Wordsworth was a man of feeling, for an Englishman, but well compared to Oor Rabbie quite frankly he was nothing to write home about. Such Passion. And such eyes! I mean, have you seen the portrait, you know the Kilmarnock Edition one, the one you see on all the ashtrays, the one on all the dishtowels . . . the absolute Spitting Image of John Cairney! He . . . Felt Things, don't you feel that?

I love a Burns Supper, don't you? Now that the Ne'erdy's by we're into the Supper Season again. It's nice a wee taste of haggis now and again, not that you'd want to eat it too often, it does tend to come back on you a wee bit, doesn't it? Not that I'm keen on neeps! A weedrop's plenty. So I thought it was nice that we in the Women's Guild declared Women's Lib this year and held our own. Well, it's better than just sitting in watching Moira Anderson yowling Caw The Yowes on the television. Sandra Peden, her that works in the Co-operative she's a Gold Medallist in Elocution you know, well wait till I tell you she came on in a long Laura Ashley nightdress carrying a Wee Willie Winkie candlestick with wee pink bedsocks and a matching pompom hat and did Holy Willie's Prayer. She brought the house down! She looked just adorable . . . and Historically Accurate too I must say. Then she came back later on in a wee Royal Stewart tartan skirt and did Wee Modest Crimson Tippet Floo'er and Tae A Moose and some of the other Guid Auld Scots Favourites.

Of course some of Our Guild Members are dare I say it just that wee bit narrow minded. It wasn't like that at my hubby's last Kirk, telling you the Young Mothers' Meeting we had there was Really Radical. But well, you have to go Where You're Called! As He says to me you can choose yir freends

6

but you canny choose yir flock! With this lot there were those who stayed at the end to tutt-tutt at some of the language and that. I just says to Mrs Sneddon that she needed a new battery for her hearing aid and that a daimen-icker in a thrave didny mean whit she thought it did! And anyway Burns had always been Very Frankly Spoken about that kind of thing. Before his time really. Of course somebody, Who Shall Be Nameless, would bring up the subject of Burns-And-You-Know-What, and how many of his children were born on The Wrong Side Of The Blanket, What Right Had We to look down on Brown Owl for her shotgun wedding when we were all supposed to look up to Rabbie Burns as Our Big Hero? I tried to tell her, don't be daft, everybody knows Artists Are Different.

Anyway, every time I hear 'Ae Fond Kiss' I Melt Inside, I really do . . .

Scotch Mist (The Scotsport Song)

Lazy Sunday Afternoon in Central Scotland.
You scoosh "Yes please"
Behind your knees
And ask him what he's got planned?
All over Central Scotland, men are pulling down the blinds.
The men of Central Scotland got something
Sort of Sunday Afternoonish on their minds.

Match of the day, action replay it's on Scotsport.
Chuck us a can, a man's not a man without Scotsport.
You can cook good, you can look good
You can play hard to get.
To turn him on's impossible —
He's turning on the set.
He'll never tell you he loves you
Unless he's pissed.
Love in a Cold Climate,
Scotch Mist!

Pissed off with life
Your average wife
Is quite entitled to feel
He's a waste of a bottle of Bad-E-Das
And a damned good Meal.
He'll say, after Scotsport
You're next on the list.
Love in a Cold Climate,
Scotch mist!

Verena: Security
(Monologue)

See since Derek went up to work up there on the Rigs things have been Different. I can't honestly say I really miss . . . Well, basically to tell you the truth it's been . . . better in a way. Definitely. Financially anyway.

I mean we'd never have been able to afford all this. See before with Derek's Other Job, before, on-shore, honest-to-god the Mortgage was a Millstone. Telling you, I thought we'd of been clomping around on the bare floor-boards and sitting on orange-boxes watching a wee black-and-white portable for ever.

But see since he went Up There — well, it's Security, isn't it. Not only did we double-glaze and fitted-Tintawn the whole place from top to bottom but I got my Dream Kitchen! The Exact Units I wanted, eye level grill, Tricity Rotisserie, fully stocked freezer, oh Derek insisted on it.

Money no object.

Not that I bother much with the cooking while he's away. You don't, for yourself, do you? And I'm out a lot, I tend to just slurp down a cup of Slimma-soup, stick a wee dollop of quiche in the microwave or something while I'm waiting for my Carmens to heat up.

Och, just round to my Mother's, basically, just to get out the house — I've never been one just to sit in listening to the Central Heating switching itself off and on. But see Derek he's that jealous! Honestly, always was, ver-near Divorce Proceedings every time I went out with emdy for a Campari after the Country Dancing . . .

But basically my mother and I have always been very close.

Although I think it's with us having the None Of A Family ourselves that I've adjusted so well. Derek was telling us only the last time he was home all about his Mate up there on the Rigs. Diver or something, honest-to-god I don't have a *clue* what they actually *do* up there, don't ask me — anyway, seems This Chap had Two Boys, one teenage, the other growing out of anoraks faster than look-at-you so She put pressure on him. How if the boys were to stay-on and get their Highers they needed the Security etc. So he took the job. Seems the Separation put a Strain on the Fragile Fabric of their Marriage and they started to Not Get On. Sexually etc.

9

Not that I can say either Derek or I have ever had any problems in the Bedroom Compartment. Touch wood. Excuse my French . . . No I can honestly say that Two Weeks On, Two Weeks Off suits me fine just as long as he minds to cut his toe-nails . . . I mean you've got to keep the Home Fires Burning, Grin and Bear it, make him Feel Welcome — although see when he's up at midnight frying eggs and he spatters grease all over my good ceramic hob I could brain him so I could — but I just tell myself he's Not Home Forever and I bite my tongue.

Anyway, this mate of his and his wife — things went from bad to worse, seems he met this woman from Dundee who travelled down regular on the same train and one day he just Got Off with her and the upshot of the whole thing was a Dear-Jeannette-Letter from Sullom Voe.

Course, as Derek says, his mate is basically a very decent bloke. Good family man. He'll make sure neither the wife nor the two boys ever want for anything.

10

Fat Girl's Confession
(Rap)

Roll up and see the Fat Lady!
Such a jolly sight to see.
Seems my figure is a Figure of Fun . . .
To everyone but me.

Smile! Say Cottage Cheese!
You all know me —
I'm the Office Fat Girl, the one you see
Wearing Vast Dark Dresses and a Cheery Veneer . . .
And lingerie constructed by a civil engineer.

Occasionally, you meet some bloke who'll give you this tripe
About how, yeuch, he's repelled by the skinny model type.
He can't see the attraction, he'll swear by all he owns
It'd be like lying in bed with a rickle of bones.
But, oh how he *lurrves*
Yir Voluptuous Curves
And your Supper Board that Groans.

I met him at my wee cousin's wedding — he was the Best Man
— he says to me would you like to go out for a bite to eat? I
mean, do you fancy a curry? A Chinese? An Italian? I said,
who me? Oh, I love . . .

Lasagne and canne-linguini and *pasta* and stuff.
(well, who with pasta, ever says basta,
enough!)
And then for my *main* course I tend to choose
something smothered in a sauce made of butter, cream and
    booze
with asparagus hollandaise and cauliflower mornay
potatoes dauphines, onion rings and mushrooms saute.
And after the cheeseboard, my sweet tooth's nagging, so
I need another great big stodgy wedge of Blackforest Gateau.
Well, when it comes to pudding,
the way I see it —
with cheesecake you've got a choice:
Either EAT it or BE it.

11

I didnae cry when he left me.
I gave not one cheep, not a chirrup —
just devoured a whole packet of Mr Kipling's Kunzle Cakes
and a half-hundredweight sack of Mexicali Taco chips dunked
    in Maplesyrup,
went for a double blackpudding supper, then half an hour
    later,
I ravished the refrigerator
(in my classic response to Rejection and Pain)
and immediately began eating
My Heart Out again.

But, Oh
Dear Joe.
much as I miss you
I just been reading how Fat Is A Feminist Issue.
Fat Girls like me have all fallen from grace —
If I could feed my own ego I wouldnae need to feed my face!
Everyone needs Oral Satisfaction, but
the Truly Fulfilled don't need a filled-full gut.
I says, Enough of this Junk Food, You Are What You Eat.
When did you last see your lover?
When did you last see your feet?
So . . . I'm persevering, but it's kind of hard
to live on lettuce, and self-regard.

But, you know, I've been really, really, really good today!
Breakfast was black coffee, plus a saccharine tab from the
    tube.
For my lunch, a half-a-cup of chicken bullion made with a
Knorr chicken stock-cube.
Dinner: two slice of starch-reduced Ryvita
with a scrape of slimmer's imitation margarine,
then I pedalled myself blue in the face on the Exercise
    Machine.
See, I've joined this Health Club, and hell, I
saw some sights you wouldnae believe!
Enough heaving flesh to make you heave.
All that pummelling, and pedalling, and pounding, and
    sweating
and keeking in the mirror to see how much thinner you're
    getting!

12

Well, there's not one lady Waging the Inch War or wielding
   the tape
who doesnae wish for a Dishy Man to lick her inty shape.

So I'm stuck here in this Stephanie Bowman Sweat-It-Off
   Slimmersuit
I feel a right clown!
I'm to huff, I'm to puff,
I'll *wear* my hips down.
I'll mortify my surplus flesh,
remove it like a tumour . . .
and all to make of myself the kind of confection
who'll appeal to the Consumer?

Look At Us
(Song)

Can't you see us in the movies?
Can't you see us play our part?
You as Charlie Chaplin
And me as the World's Sweetheart.
Hearts and flowers and baggy pants
In flickering black and white
My dumbshow love and cupid's bow —
But the captions don't read right.
Can't understand what's happening
Imagine how it feels
To be stuck in a Saturday serial —
And someone's switched the reels.
And I'm bound and gagged on the Railway Line —
Is this the final shot?
The piano's playing overtime
To catch up with the plot —
And the train is getting nearer
My wide eyes open and shut
Surely this can't be quite right —
Should someone not shout Cut!?

>   *Oh* look at us,
>   Don't we look ridiculous?

In the musicals of the Thirties
We make the Perfect Pair.
We click together in any kind of weather
like Rogers and Astaire.
Fine Romance or Ziegfeld Folly?
Tapshoes, top hat and tails —
Oh you look real cute in your morningsuit,
and I'm polished to the nails.
As Just One of the Chorus
good timing's all you need
Oh I'd be fine if you hadn't pulled me out of line
To dance your female lead.

>   *Oh* look at us,
>   Don't we look ridiculous?

I saw this Forties' movie
That could of been 'bout us —
Like he kissed her then she slapped him —
then he gave her hair a muss.
"I've paid you your retainer —
Now find him that's your brief!"
"Is that a dress you're nearly wearin'
Or a Lurex handkerchief?"
So let us drink to the long cool blonde
and the lonely private dick
Who conversed in whiplash wisecracks
That cut them to the quick.
There was a loner and a
lady schoolmarm, and she turned gangster's moll.
But in the end *they* solved it —
So it wasn't like *us* at all.
So, pour me another bourbon,
I'll drink to all we did,
though outside it's still raining,
here's looking at us, kid!

Oh look at us
Don't we look ridiculous.

Phyllis Marlowe:
Only Diamonds Are Forever
(Monologue)

The letters lying there on the mat didn't exactly look as though if I didn't open them the world would stop. I picked them up. I turned them over, squinting through the bloodshot marblings of my hangover and the tangled remains of last night's Twiggy eyelashes. It was back in sixty-six. Those days the world was a more innocent place. I fanned out the fistful of manilla in my mitt. As I had thought. Zilch. A final demand from the Gas Board and a threat from Glasgow Public Libraries if I didn't return *The Maltese Falcon* and pay my seventeen-and-six fine they'd permanently withdraw my ticket and cut my left hand off. And what was this? I swallowed. I swallowed again. An appointment card, report today, today at two-thirty, the Brook Clinic, a discreet logo and address, a classy address in the city's ritzy West End.

I showered, shaved — shaved my legs — like I said this was back in sixty-six, the world was a more innocent place, those days no one accused you of anti-feminism if you were caught with a tube of Immac. I sniffed. I showered again.

I emerged from the bathroom a half an hour later in a cloud of Amplex Aerosol avalanched in Boots' 365 Talcum. The place looked like the ski-slopes at Chamonix.

I shimmied shivering to the bedsit, slotted another shilling in the gas fire and reached for the knob on the third drawer of the tallboy. I knew exactly what I was looking for, they had to be here somewhere, the one and only pair of knickers left uncontaminated in that disastrous load at the launderette, the stuff that had got washed along with that bargain-price bright-pink non-fast Indian-cotton mini-skirt from C&A. Some bargain, huh? These days I peeked out at the world through unevenly rose-tinted underwear.

I found them at last..Virgin white as the day they crossed the counter at Galls. I slid them on. Two-thirty, huh? I showered again .

Two-twenty-five found me on the steps of a slightly crumbling mansion in what the Estate Agents would call a highly desirable residential area. A simple brass plaque spelt out Brook Advisory Clinic. The whole place screamed Anonymity.

I pressed the bell. The door creaked open a couple of inches.

"Yes?" said a voice more frosted than its glass panels. I showed her my card.

"Two-thirty," I barked.

She barked back, the door slid open wide enough for me to enter and I found myself in a roomful of dames all with rigor mortis of the third-finger-of-the-left-hand. Engagement rings. Woolworth's engagement rings, each a lump of glass as big as the Ritz. There was more imitation ice than in *The Ancient Mariner*, more gilt than in a psychiatrist's office, more rolled gold than in Acapulco.

Tonight these dames were going to have greener fingers than Percy Thrower.

Each broad had a Tame Boyfriend with her, like a poodle on a lead. All you could see of any of them was a pair of very pink ears sticking out behind old copies of the *Woman's Own*. Nobody in the place looked exactly relaxed.

I sat down. Dame opposite was wearing laddered black Beatle nylons — Jesus, nobody had worn Beatle nylons since sixty-four Chrissakes. She was reading *The Uses of Literacy*. Maybe she did have an honours degree in sociology, but she certainly was sixpence short in the shilling when it came to dress-sense. Still, somebody loved her. Otherwise she wouldn't be here. I slid my eyes over the gent she had accessorising her. Below magazine-level at any rate he was not painful to look at.

Over in the corner behind a gigantic desk sat this old bird who looked as though she had been there since Marie Stopes was pre-pubescent.

"Next!" she plainsonged and fixed me with an old-fashioned look from behind her lorgnette.

I sidled over. "Name," she stated.

"Marlowe," I quipped. "Marlowe with an 'e'. Phyllis Marlowe. 'Ph' for Phellatio, 'Y' for Yesplease, 'L' for Love, 'L' for Leather, 'I' for Intercourse, 'S' for —"

She looked at me as though I had said a dirty word.

"In here," she said, "remove tights and pants, lie up on that table. Doctor will be here to examine you directly." She pronounced it like Doktor with a "k". I gulped. I must pull myself together. I loosened my waistband and pulled myself together.

I found myself in a rough cubicle with a torn curtain hanging to approximately knee-height. Through this, various bits of anonymous female gooseflesh and, in the ringing tones of a Roedean Gymmistress, Doktor's voice interrogating the bimbo-next-door about the ins-and-outs of her sexlife. The whole place was about as private as Grand Central Station on Glasgow Fair Saturday.

Five minutes later found me flinching and clenching, biting into the black vinyl of the couch as cold steel penetrated. I spat out a curse.

Ten minutes after that — I sat in triumph, six precious months supply of the pill in my grasp.

Doktor wagged a metronome finger at me.

"You must take for twenty-one days religiously, stop for seven, always begin on the same day of the week, got it? Now, what do you do?"

"I'm a student at Jordanhill college doing Fribble," I riposted.

She gave me a look, I returned it, she slammed it back, I caught it neatly, spun round and delivered a deft backward glance over my left shoulder.

Back in the waiting room it had gotten twice as crowded. Obviously there was a future in this business, they'd hit a nerve somewhere.

Then I saw him. Shoulder-length blond hair, embroidered cheese-cloth shirt, single strand of beads — I mean, beads but *tasteful* — a sensual hint of hash and patchouli, and midnight blue denims stretched taut then flaring over the longest, leanest bass-guitarist's thighs in Glasgow. Like, this guy's loons had *style*. I'd loved him for as long as I could remember. I'd have known him anywhere..

"Haw, thingmy," he jack-knifed to his feet. "Whit urr you daeing here?"

"I might ask you the same question."

His Adam's apple slid up and down his throat like the lift in the Red Road Flats oughta, but don't.

"Hey, listen doll, great to see you, oh aye. Hiv tae git you roon tae wir new flat in Wilton Street, listen to a few albums, smoke a few joints, Fat Freddy's got some Moroccan in, really good stuff . . . toodle-oo!" he gabbled.

I looked over his shoulder. Coming towards him, big smile freezing fast, was this Julie Christie lookalike in Fringed Suede.

I smiled a lopsided smile. "So long Blue-Eyes, see you around."

Outside it was still raining. On my way through Kelvingrove Park I flipped my once-precious packet into a wastebasket and walked on.

Last I saw, a couple of hand-in-hand schoolkids had fished them out and were avidly reading the instruction leaflet. Probably disappointed to find it wasn't twenty-one tabs of acid. Sex is wasted on the young.

Back in my bedsit, I spooned bitter instant into my Union-Jack-I'm-Backing-Britain mug — this was sixty-six, the world was a more innocent place — and sighed. I guessed I'd just have to swallow it strong and hot and black and bitter, I'd run clean out of Marvel. I ripped the cellophane off another packet of chocolate digestives.

The Suzanne Valadon Story
(Rap)

I could of been a laundress,
a soft-soaped hopeless scrubber —
I could of been a waitress —
And lived to Serve Anothair?
I could of been a housemaid
and stayed upon my knees —
Instead of these
Because Moi — sans chemise—
was cer-tain to please
Until I used my noddle
I was the Bohemienne
comedienne
Who is an artist's model!

I'd be flat on my ass still
If I hadn't seized zee pastel
I was just a girl who couldaint say Non!
Now I am the artiste, Suzanne Valadon!

Mon affaire with Renoir
Deed not go very far
And Lautrec, although nice
Seemply could not reach my heights
Edouard Manet — he canny!
(Quel *type*,What a creep!)
But Dégas,
Oh-la-la
he drew me in ink and he etched me on zinc
Until some bloody Fauve went and painted me mauve
and Seurat stippled me pink.

Oh they did me in oils
Till I came out in boils
but when I asked them for a crayon,
Oh they turned me Van Gogh's ear . . .

I'd be posing noon till ten still
If I hadn't snatched zee pencil
I was the girl who couldaint say Non!
Now I'm an artiste, Suzanne Valadon.

Then I'd climb in zee sack
for the price of a cognac
Oh life in Bohemia
Could not 'ave been more seamier.
But I'd have slept with them for sables —
Zee brushes not zee furs!

I was well on my way
To the Salon des Refusés
I was just a girl who couldaint say Non!
Now I'm la grande artiste,
Suzanne Valadon.

Oh, I was seeck, seeck, seeck
being scribbled, screwed or blitzed
At the Moulin de la Galette
So I told them what to do with
Zee impressionist palette
I got off the dais,
I covered my ass,
snapped his charcoal stick in two
And I drew
without a fuss
Aha!
said Renoir
I see you're One of Us.
And Lautrec (I'll always *lov* heem)
Said wis-out a doubt Suzanne
You can be dronk in charge of a charcoal line
As good as any man.
Dégas said I was a genius
and on further inspection
Put heez monnaie where his mouth was.
And bought mes pictures
to grace heez great collection.

I'd have ended in zee guttair as a clapped out lush
Eef I hadn't seized mon courage and a number seven brush
I was the girl who couldaint say Non!
Now I am la Grande Artiste
Moi!
Suzanne Valadon.

Vymura: The Shade Card Poem

Now artistic I aint, but I went to choose paint
'cos the state of the place made me sick.
I got a shade card, consumers-aid card, but it stayed hard to
   pick
So I asked her advice as to what would look nice,
would blend in and not get on my wick.

She said 'our Vymura is super in Durer,
or see what you think of this new shade, Vlaminck.
But I see that you're choosy . .
Picasso is newsy . . that's greyish-greeny-bluesy . .
Derain's all the rage . .
that's hot-pink and Fauve-ish . .
There's Monet . . that's mauve-ish . .
And Schwitters,
that's sort-of-a *beige*.'

She said 'Fellow next door just sanded his floor
and rollered on Rouault and Rothko
His hall, och it's Pollock an' he
did his lounge in soft Hockney
with his cornice picked out in Kokoshka.'

'Now avoid the Van Gogh, you'll not get it off,
the Bonnard is bonny,
you'd be safe with matt Manet,
the Goya is *gorgeous*
or Chagall in eggshell,
but full-gloss Lautrec's sort of tacky.
So stick if you can to satin-finish Cezanne
or Constable . . that's kind of Khaki.
Or the Gainsborough green . .
and I'd call it hooey to say Cimabue
would never tone in with Soutine.'

23

'If it looks a bit narrow when you splash on Pissarro
one-coat Magritte covers over.'
She said 'this Hitchens is a nice shade for kitchens
with some Ernst to connect 'em at other end of the spectrum
Botticelli's lovely in the louvre.'
She said 'If it was mine I'd do it Jim Dine . .
don't think me elitist or snobby . .
but Filipo Lippi'd
look awfy insipid,
especially in a large-ish lobby!'

Well, I did one wall Watteau, with the skirting Giotto
and the door and the pelmet in Poussin.
The ceiling's de Kooning,
other walls all in Hals
and the whole place looks quite . . . cavalier,
with the woodwork in Corot —
but I think tomorrow
I'll flat-white it back to Vermeer.

Franglais
(Rap)

I should have had the savoir faire
To find out who you were
Before our affaire
Avait commencé.
Before I got turned on
by the Dom Perignon
I should have stopped to penser.

Ha Ha! Qui Moi? Tu m'aimes? Pourquoi?

Should have had more sang froid.
The night we enjoyed
What Freud
called the Auld Alliance.
Known your sexy joie de vivre
was toujours half seas ivre
a mere alcoholic compliance.

Ha Ha! Qui Moi? Tu m'aimes? Pourquoi?

Nouveau Beaujolais is thrilling
and Calvados is chilling.
The spirit makes you willing —
but it hampers . . .
The only objét trouvé
I could find under your duvet
was encore une bouteille de champers.

Ha Ha! Qui Moi? Tu m'aimes? Pourquoi?

If we hadn't mixed the grape and grain
we'd per'aps have come again
(amour is main-
ly for the frisky)
Oh, we'd've been tête a tête yet
If I hadn't let
you pour the nineteenth le scotch whisky.

Ha Ha! Qui Moi? Tu m'aimes? Pourquoi?

So I must say Au Revoir —
Tout fed up with Pas-Ce-Soir
I've-'ad-Far-Too-Much-to-Boire,
Josephine.
If we'd only stuck to Perrier . . .
You'd have loved me more and merrier
If that Vat Soixante-Neuf had not been
so beau . . . beauc . . .beaucoup your scene!

Cowboys and Priests
(Song)

The lady said men could be divided
Into cowboys and priests
But she was not so hot at spotting
The difference between men and beasts.
She was prone to such confusion
It twisted her in knots —
She said mark well, you just can't tell
A leopard by its spots.
Yet they said men could be divided
Into cowboys and priests.

Oh, after their devotions
He'd prayed to be released
When he looked beyond her
To the wide blue yonder
Was he cowboy then, or priest?
Oh, she was tired and had taken to declining
All invitations to feasts
Due to the confusion
Between cowboys and priests.

She said along would come some cowboy
When your whole soul cried for a priest
She was tired of being surprised by a wind from the west
When her weathercock pointed east.
Oh, he'd want to hear her confession
And to leave her feeling blessed
So she'd see a sheep in wolf's clothing
As all her love went west.
Yes every man can be divided
Part cowboy, part priest.

27

Six Men Monologues

No. 1: Annemarie.

Men see men I've had it
Up to here absolutely
It's all off completely.
I said suppose that'll suit you fine I said
You can go out with your mates
Every night of the week and not just Thursdays
I said,
Look at the state of you
The beer's all going to your belly already
And coming from the West of Scotland you
Are statistically unlikely
even to reach the age of 25
without false teeth
And to tell the truth
Since we got engaged
You never bother with the Brut
or the good suit I said
I'm sick to the backteeth of
Every time we go for a Chinese
You order
chicken and chips, fried egg and peas.
I said No way
Believe me the only way I'd ever consider
The World Cup in Mala-bloody-ga
For my honeymoon
Is if I was guaranteed
An instant trade you in for a
Six foot shit-hot sharp shooter that never failed to hit the spot.
I told him where to stick his bloody
One carrot diamond-is-forever.

I blame his mother.

No. 2: Pamela.

Men, my boyfriend says, Honest-to-God he says men huvn't got it any easier than women these days! He says men aren't any more sure and secure within their own sexual identity. Oh naw, not by a long, long chalk. And yiv got tae watch not tae laugh at them, huvn't yi. Everybody knows if yi laugh at a man in That Way he will wilt for ever, willn't he?

I was reading this article in a Playboy Magazine round at my boyfriend's place, or was it Penthouse, anyway, I seem to be spending quite a lot o' time round at my boyfriend's reading magazines and here it says how these several top U.S. psychiatrists had done this survey on how your emotions can sabotage your sexlife even if you *are* a man and here it blamed the sexually aggressive female of the seventies for the sexual recession of the eighties. No, apparently it's world wide. Even in Italy these days women are failing to feel the pinch. The article says there was a definite swing away from swinging and back to the values of the fifties. Apparently people are even going back to the fifties contraceptives! Supposed to be that this whole you know, Ronald Reagan, Swing-to-the-Right, Fun-Fashion, Fifties thing disny stop at the glitter-sox the roll-ons and the lurex! It says people were turning again to the old tried and true spices of Guilt and Feeling Dirty and Furtiveness And Stuff in a frantic attempt to resurrect the whole sad affair.

My boyfriend says that ladies like me huv been just too liberated for our own good. Just you mark my words, he says, the Worm Will Turn.

No. 3: Judith.

Men said the small ad in the wants column
am I expecting too much
lady fifty one tall shapely separated
genuine gregarious aware
varied interests vegetarian (own muesli-mix)
New Statesman reader romantic sincere
Wishes to share

simple sunshine and undemanding companionship
(view marriage) with
comfortable mature strong nonsmoker sincere
adventurous male graduate music-lover (radius Hampstead
    ten miles)
Whole life spent searching for him.
Lady seeks soulmate (or sim.)

No. 4: Kimberley.

Men said the Cosmogirl (eyes
lighting up like dollarsigns in Vegas)
Men And How To Hook Them by Tamara Gogetter M.D.
Sip your dulep,
slick another coat of Golddigger Red on your fingernails,
Now Read On . . .
"A good substitute for a silverspoon is a
castiron nerve and wherever the Beautiful People are
Be There —
even if you have to hock your last
Hermes scarf to raise the fare.
(P.S. spas are passé and so is San Trop).
Consider Best Bars as a first resort,
regard the single cocktail you'll shell out for as
sheer investment, get yourself
gift wrapped, send for our jetset silklook shirt,
rid yourself of
even that inch-of-pinch and the
body beautiful will be guaranteed bait for
ace race driver or millionaire financier in advanced stages of
    senility.
(Offer subject to availability.)

No. 5: Mo.

Men says My Boss
are definitely more dependable
and though even in these days of equal pay
men tend to come a wee bitty more expensive
due to the added responsibility a man tends to have

in his jobspecification
Well for instance you can depend on a man not to get
pregnant.
My Boss says men are more objective.
Catch a man bitching
about healthhazards and conditions
and going out on strike over no papertowels in the toilet
or nagging over the lack of day nursery facilities
My Boss says as far as he's concerned a crêche is a motor
    accident in Kelvinside
and any self respecting woman should have a good man
to take care of her so its only pinmoney anyway
and that's bound to come out in the attitude.
Well a man isn't subject to moods
or premenstrual tension a guy
isn't going to phone in sick with some crap about cramps.
My Boss says a man rings in
with an upset stomach and you know either
he means a hangover or else his brother
managed to get him a ticket for Wembley.

You know where you are with a man.

No. 6: Bette.

Men said the housewife
(Waiting for the coffee to perk)
Honestly, Muriel, men!
(Wringing her apron in mock indignation)
That's the third time this week I've picked his
Good polyester-dacron trousers up off the floor and
Hung them up in their crease.
What's the use?
Doesn't lift a finger, does David
Never a handsturn from him, believe me.
The kitchenette is a closed book.
Don't you be downtrodden Muriel.
Make that clear from the start.

Men, honestly, wee boys at heart.
Men!

Mean Mr Love
(Song)

I'm Sal, I sell
haberdashery
(while floorwalkers walk the floor)
at Armour and Love, Limited's
big department store.
When customers come crowding
or when the times is hard
through Christmas rush and Summer slack
I sell it by the yard.

Still, I'd be silly
to think I'm safe
because I earn an honest buck.
The streets these days are full of girls
who're right down on their luck.
So I'm sure to always look busy
and never have time to kill —
No — it's not just a matter of not getting caught
With your fingers in the till.

Because,
Mean Mr Love,
he'll give you the sack,
he'll kiss your arse
to your face
and kick you in the teeth behind your back.

Mr Love, he asked me
out dancin'.
Man, but that guy was Bad News
From the top of his curled Fedora
to his Co-Respondent shoes.
I said, "If old Mr Armour he finds out
he won't be too pleased,
he doesn't like you getting friendly
with the employees."

No, I won't dilly-dally
down the Primrose Path,
won't throw my cap at the moon
Don't wanna be left holding
the baby all too soon.
Because I love him don't mean he'll love me back
the way that I deserve.
The girl who hooks a rich man
got to keep some bait in reserve.

Because,
Mean Mr Love,
the moment you hit the sack,
he'll kiss your arse
to your face
and kick you in the teeth behind your back.

Maintenance Man
(Song)

Couldn't get to sleep last night
for the drippin' of the tap
Hurt my head just to lie in bed
Wishing it would stop
Phoned the man and I asked would he fix it
But the bastard never came
So I'm left with my fury wondering who to blame.

Chorus
Oh, do-it-yourself has limits
But I'll do all I can
To try and get by to try and get by
Without my maintenance man.

Couldn't get to sleep last night
For thinking how you'd gone
I turn and toss over the loss
Of the one my sun shone on
Phoned you up and I begged you to come over
But you bastard you never came
So I'm stuck with all this leftover love
Now you don't feel the same.

Chorus
Oh do-it-yourself has limits
But I'll do all I can
To be freed of the need
For my maintenance man.

Mae: Come Up and See Me Sometime
(Monologue)

Come up and
see me
sometime. I feel
recently you've had a glum time.
So come and see me,
drink up my Duty Free.

Come up and see me sometime —
I asked him casually,
it makes no odds to me —
if he should see me —
assuming I'm free
sometime.

What, the place is a palace?
That's not
so unusual, is it?
Especially when I've got a friend who might
come up and visit.
No, honestly,
I often sit in alone
wearing a bottle and a half of Christmas cologne.

Wasn't easy
to get the desired effect
in this god-awful room —
Squeezy-mopped the lino,
gave the white fur rug a groom,
stuck my hair in heated rollers,
kind-of-casual-but-vamp,
threw an Indian headsquare
over the landlady's lamp,
lit a couple of joss-sticks
to drown out the cat,
everything to spell a welcome
short of writing on the mat —
You should of
seen me half an hour ago,
like a geisha in my facepack

Casually trailing something black
and sort of flimsy over the chairback.

Ask a man to dinner in your bedsit
and after you're fed
there's nowhere to sit,
except on the bed.
Well, ask a
gentleman friend to whatsit in your bedsit
and after an hour and a half
of batting your eyelids at him
you begin to suspect it's more than
the lighting that's dim.
Well, just because a lady
temporarily
hasn't got a man beside her
there's no reason to treat her like a
black widow spider.

So your lady's left you . . .
My man's left me.
Who would it hurt if we let ourselves be led
via tea and
sympathy to
booze and bed?

Where's your hat?
Where's your hurry?
What are the thanks for?
I've always got plenty of instant
coffee and rapport . . .

Maybe he was shy.
Maybe it's a blessing.
Polite goodnights and then
'Why don't you come up again . . .
anytime you're passing.'

36

Liz Lochhead's Lady Writer Talkin' Blues
(Rap)

Woke up this morning to Familiar Pain
It seemed mah lover had left me 'gain
Oh I felt like cryin' so I had me a session
And I hugged mah pillah with its You Shaped Depression
I liked that
Some pun
Nice Ring to it—
Sounded Good.

So I dried mah eyes and examined mah pain
Felt cayerfully all over mah feelings again
So I called up Mah Muse and I tried to bribe it
To provide the Right Phrase to Describe it
Then I got it.
Brokain-Hearted.

So I dived out of bed to jot it down right
Had too many good notions run off in the night
Honey, when we was happy never wrote me a page
Typewriter stayed covered as the budgie cage
Not a cheep from it.

He said he had a new lover she was still at school
She might be dumb but she was beautiful
And if he'd caused me Pain, well
He was sure it'd pass.
I said the Main Pain was A Pain In The Ass.

Oh I went at it, toothed and nailed
Then tearful, asked him
Where I'd failed
Came on more tragic than a full Greek Chorus
I hurled every cliché in Roget's Thesaurus
I threw the book at him
Then the teaset —
Said plenty
I've given you the best six months of mah life
Never darken mah door again
That kinda thing
Em barrassing.

He said I'd always relished scenes
supposed I was dyin' to spill the beans
get all mah Hot Passion down in Cold Print
It was all good material I'd make me a mint —
Grist to the Mill.

He said that now he'd 'scaped Mah Hooks
He was prepared for me to Cook The Books
For the slander and the lies, any 'mount
That I'd dredge up to dress my 'count
Said talk about Castration and The Written Word
The Pen is Mightier than the Sword
He knew all about it
Too right!

He said Mah Work was a load a' drivel
I called it detail, he called it trivial
Tappin' out them poems in mah tacky room
About mah terrible cramps and mah
Moon Trawled Womb —
Women's trouble?
Self Pity.

He said I was woolly in my politics
And personal poetry gave him the icks
He couldn't do His Brainwork in the same house as me
Because I screwed up his objectivity
So he'd be off now, just because . . .
And who the f-f-fantasy did I think I was,
Dorothy Parker?

Well I haven't seen him since, well I never thought I would
And the last three weeks haven't been too good
Between the not sleeping and the boozing and the cryin'
And wallowing in the works of Edna O'Brien . . .
But someday soon I'll say enough is enough.
And I'll set myself down to Write Him Off.

Page Three Dollies
(Rap)

We're the Page Three Dollies
And you think that we're Exploited?
Well who is screwing who?
Frankly darling I'm delighted
If Mr Commuter's Pulse Goes Up
And his eyelid flickers.
At the photo of me with my thumbs hooked in my knickers.
When you read me on your way to work
And I can raise a smile,
Frankly, darling, they make it all worthwhile
And we're laughing all the way to the bank.

We provide anaesthetic sex
To numb your mind
For the daily bump and grind
We grease the wheels of commerce
Lubricate machinery
Captains of industry know ogling at me
Is better for the workforce than bromide in their tea
And they're laughing all the way to the bank.

We never get the credit
The public don't deserve us
The way I look at it we're a public service
I reckon we keep the nation's quotient of pleasure up —
Let's face it Mrs Average is unlikely quite to measure up
And if you keep my pic in mind
As you go through the motions
Of the marriage bed's
Twice weekly devotions
Well the wife is none the wiser,
She's got us to thank . . .
And we're laughing all the way to the bank?

Though they sometimes fudge our edges
And airbrush our pimples
Tape up our tits and round out our dimples
They touch up our pubes
And whittle down our waists
Till they imagine we appeal to your ideal tastes
And they're laughing all the way to the bank.

As long as it isn't *your* wife
As long as it's not your daughter
Getting her cheesecloth shirt drenched
With a bucket of water —
Don't think that we're indecent,
Not a bit
We're more rosy aureole
Than perked-up clit,
But they're laughing all the way to the bank.

What you read in the paper
Might make you see red
If you were less distracted by
My centrefold spread
Though my news value's scanty,
I'm sure you'll agree
If you look hard enough
On page twenty three
You'll find half a paragraph
On World War Three —
But they're laughing all the way to the bank.

Feminine Advice
(Rap)

Like every other mother, mine
was keen to tell her daughter
to certainly go swimming, but
to not go near the water.
To find myself a Good Career
to Travel and Have Fun
and not to tie myself down at eighteen with husband, home
and bloody ungrateful children
like she'd done.
If I cut according to my cloth and didn't
get excited
at around thirty I would find myself miraculously
Mister-Righted.
She said to watch my handbag and keep myself nice.

Oh I sure was grateful for the feminine advice.

But I had a lot to learn when I went to school —
like how women weren't
mechanically minded as a rule.
Headmaster, careers mistress, in subtle alliance
to remind us we were rotten at Maths and Science.
Oh, I really shocked her
when I told her, 'Miss,
I want to be a doctor' —
She asked me had I thought it out? A woman could do worse
than be a nurse.
And "in fact, with dedication, any bright girl can
be the driving force behind a really Top Man
(and once you've got him, here's how to please —
via his stomach and macaroni surprise)
oh, he'll put you on a pedestal,
he'll treat you like a queen
if you just put your trust
in Pristine Clean —
remember in Office Practise the thing that is most shocking
is turning up with black-rim nails, or splashes in your stocking.
So, when you go for interview,
Knees together in navyblue,

42

Wear little white collars and be quiet as mice . . .''

Oh I sure was grateful for the feminine advice.

And those Women's Mags were always telling you
about thrush, the hot flush and what to do
and how to keep your husband true
and what to dip in your fondue.
How to address Royalty (with the minimum of slanging)
How to unravel old potscourers and torn tights and
Knit them up into an Attractive Wallhanging.
How New Ways With Eyeshadow turn a housewife to a teaser.
How to tan, bake a flan, and plan for your freezer.
How to rescue junkshop finds and strip them for Good Use.
And, especially for Christmas,
Sauce for the goose.
Oh, their serving suggestions sounded awfully nice,

So I sure was grateful for the feminine advice.

But I'm aware and now I know
that men are overrated.
I've cast my simpers, found myself,
I'm Spare-Rib liberated.
I fly above False Consciousness
I love me more, I love him less
I use Real Words for parts of me
Which formerly I hated.
The day when Women Seize the Night
will only come much nearer when
male doctors get it together
and invent a pill for men.
But if we're stuck with contraception
as sure as eggs is eggs
Don't conform to sexist fancies —
refuse to shave your legs.

Oh, the Answer to Cancer
and the end of Tyranny and Terror
is self-help coffee mornings
with your speculum and mirror.
So,
I followed the Y.B.A. wife campaign,
decided to never get spliced
And I sure am grateful for the feminine advice

Yes, I really am grateful for the feminine advice.

Sharon: Incest
(Monologue)

I'm doing the Bronte Heroes at school, for my Sixth Year Studies dissertation.

It was Mr Fleming's idea.

It's quite a good subject though — I mean, I was reading this serial in my Mum's Woman's Own, all about this governess and this French Comte who was . . . dead Dark, and Moody, and Mysterious and completely copied from Mr Rochester! I mean, they had a big influence, the Brontes, right up as far as modren days, no doubt about it.

It was an absolute sin for the Bronte Sisters but! Imagine being stuck in a Manse in the middle of all those moors with a minister for a father and that Mad Artist brother Bramwell — he was really *mental*, an opiate-eater, and an alcoholic and everything. Mr Fleming said it moulded their minds: Madness and the Moors.

Mr Fleming says 'Wuthering Heights' is all about incest. See, mibbe Heathcliffe was Kathy's father's illegitimate son that he brought back to be brung up with his Respectable Family. So they were half-brother and sister. Mibbe.

Mr Fleming just said it straight out in class. Incest. He's dead nice, Mr Fleming, just treats you like an adult; see once you're in the Sixth Year, you could say Anything to him.

He even invited us round to the house one night, to give me a loan of a book on the Gothic Imagination. He's not far, he lives round in the Bought Houses, that estate . . . you know, Spam Valley Dad calls it . . . it was really gorgeous, Mr Fleming's house, well not particularly from the *outside*. But, see inside, it was really Brilliant, the living room had, you know, these giant bean-bags out of Habitat, and Millions of books. I mean, one wall was practically nothing but Orange Paperback Spines. I'd love that, so I would.

I mean, it was . . . dead Lived-In. There were, you know, wee bits of Lego, and a broken Action Man and that — must have belonged to wee Steven, that's Mr Fleming's wee boy, he's only about three, I saw him with Mr Fleming in Woolworth's in Sauchiehall Street last Saturday, and he's absolutely *gorgeous*. The Spitting Image. All the same, I think Mrs Fleming might've tidied up. Especially if she knew somebody was coming.

Mrs Fleming's . . . well, she's quite fat, and she looks a lot older than Mr Fleming — not that I think he's about to do a Mr Rochester, stick her up the Loft nor nothing!

Mr Fleming had Denims on. He looked totally different than what he does at school. Really casual. He just said, 'Come away in, Sharon, and would you like a wee sherry?' He said, 'Jessie, this is Sharon, I'm sure I've told you all about her, she's one of our Star Sixth Years, all about her dissertation. She's our brightest hope for the Bursary Comp.'

So, she starts quizzing me and I start nattering on about the bloody Brontes — I think Mrs Fleming must've been really intelligent when she was young, honest-to-god she was firing them at me faster than Bamber Gascoigne, she says to me: 'And tell me, Karen, how are you going to deal with the themes of Repressed Sexuality in the Brontes' work?'

I didn't know where to look! I just sat there on that bloody Sag Bag picking bits of Farley's out of the corduroy and wishing it would open up and the polystyrene granules would swallow me!

She said, she turned to Mr Fleming and she said, 'Darling, do you mind when we were up at the Uni, and that . . . What's-His-Name, English lecturer, second year, that course on the Nineteenth Century Novel . . . remember how he was always wittering on about Incest in Wuthering Heights?'

Mr Fleming said, 'Darling, is this not your Yoga Night?'

Mrs Fleming said, 'Weight Watchers, and no, not tonight, Sweetheart, I'm right on Target.'

She said anyway she was away to make a wee cup of tea and did I take sugar?

I just sat there. As soon as she brung the tray through, I just drank it, took the book and bolted.

He's really . . . I mean, he's dead nice, Mr Fleming. Really . . . intense, even though he's got blond hair.

I mean, can you imagine Heathcliffe with blond hair?

Telephone Song

Hi there, thought I would call you
(Why Why did I pick up the telephone)
I'm fine just wondring . . . how are you
(Swore blind not to touch the telephone)

I've nothing new to say
Things've been OK
With me
Without you

Last time I phoned
You were not alone
Love lost lines crossed
Should have known

Midnight your time, six a.m. mine
All night trying to reach you
Time is up and I'm all strung up and we're too
Hung up to hang up the telephone

Why why did I call you up
(Can't touch you on the telephone)
Long distance loving's got to stop
Cut off by the telephone.

Alarm Clock Song

Excuse me, baby, I'm a
Little bit overwound.
You screw me up so tightly
Then you sleep so sound.
But
Rather than alarm you
Oh I'd charm you were I able
With my perfect bedside manner
I'd sit on your bedside table
With the moonlight
With my hands over my face
Yes I certainly do know my place.

Lying awake
Headache. Heartbreak.
My mind ticking over. I'm very calm.
I'm giving you fair warning
I'll go off some fine morning
Just like the time bomb I am.

Excuse me, baby, I'm a
Trifle overwound.
You screw me up so tightly,
Then you sleep so sound
But
Rather than alarm you
Oh I'd charm you were I able
With my perfect bedside manner
With my scarcely noticeable
With my nearly
Non-existent nervous tick.
And my breathing very light and quick.

Oh I'll get my own back
Tomorrow I'll pack
All my courage and my last fond hope.
Listen, here's my last warning
I'll go off some fine morning
Maybe that'll wake you up.

Clover
(Rap)

I'm into domesticity
Honey I'm in clover
Hovering with a dustpan and
Grooving with the hoover
I'm cleaning out my room and
It'll soon pass muster
With my elbow grease
And my feather duster
I'm brushing off my gloom and though I
Don't want to harp it
Does look rather better since
I swept you under the carpet.
Yes I'm
Into domesticity
Lover I'm in clover
Hovering with the dustpan
Grooving with the hoover.
Though I'm
Stuck here in the kitchen its
More than pots I'm stirring
Those saucy plots are thickening and
Fantasies are whirring.
Oh don't think I don't miss you 'cos
I do awfully
But hopes of someone new keep
Rising with my soufflé
No I'm far from brokenhearted though it
Was fun lover
But I'll be able to get things done
Now its over.
These days its self fulfilment time
Though so far I find . . .
Well maybe I'll get started when
I get you out of my mind.

Mealticket Song

Me and my old flame came wining-and-dining
At this restaurant.
He handed me the menu with a flourish
And he asked me what did I want.

Zipping in and out of our blue jeans —
All Summer naked and free —
So what was this with his new sharp suit?
It cut no ice with me.

He tried to look me in the eye,
Say I didn't look a day older.
Hunting madly for the Right Note to strike,
Getting colder.

Nothing
Less likely to start sparks flying
Than a burnt-out flame.
You're both in the dark
About why you ever came —
But
Thank you for my dinner, I'm
So full up it hurts,
I adored the hors d'oeuvre
But lets skip the just desserts.

Tonight I'm sitting at the same table,
Dolled-up from top-to-toe.
And I've a new man handing me the menu.
Tonight, you're my brand new beau.

But when the waiter smiles at me
You needn't look so surprised.
I've graced this place many times before
So I'm bound to be recognised.

50

Don't drum your hands on the tablecloth, darling —
Sooner or later
The Course of Time it'll arrive
On the rattling dumbwaiter.

Nothing
Less likely to last for ever
Than a brand new beau.
So, with both our eyes
Wide-open, we come and we go.
But
Thank you for my dinner, I'm
So full up it hurts.
I adored the hors d'oeuvre
But lets skip the just desserts.

Gentlemen Prefer Blonds
(Parody: Tune of 'Diamonds Are Forever')

I knew I had to have him but he wouldn't get the message
Though I beamed out telepathic bonds
I batted my eyelids but . . . Not A Sausage —
I somehow had to shake him up
And make the fancy take him up.
My hairdresser said
He could sort out my head
With Pure Henna and feathery fronds
He would tie-dye and twist me
Till no guy could resist me —
Seems gentlemen prefer blondes.

He guaranteed results with a perm that was pricey
(It got crimped round these Magic Wands)
To attract Mr Nice, hey Crazy Color's dicey —
To go shocking pink
You'd think would surely make him blink.
And though Punk Green
May be fit to be seen
'S not a flag to which this chappy responds
For from Harlow to Monroe
To Bardot, Wise Gals Know
That gentlemen prefer blondes.

He was *friendly* and stuff
but that wasn't enough
There was This Barrier we never got beyond.
So I decided to dare all —
Now I owe my all to Clairol
Just in case the gentleman prefers me Blonde.

Then this Other Guy moved in with him (don't think it was his
    brother)
He was slender and tender and bronzed.
It seemed that my chap was wrapped up in Another —
An absolute Adonis, hell
No wonder he didn't phone us, well!
Oh nothing is worse
Than to flog a dead horse
The penny dropped and finally it dawned.
A sun-streaky beach boy
With a bum like a peach, boy
The gentleman does prefer a blond!

I should be back in my pram
Dumb Blonde that I am —
It was sheer self deception had me conned!
I hope he and his chappy
Will be very happy
Because he evidently prefers a blond.

Curtains
(Song)

Woke up in your sleeping bag
Lying on the floor.
They're tearing our house down love
Can't live here anymore.
Furniture gone,
Suitcases packed
And stacked up in the hall.
Waiting for the ball and chain
Come crashing through the wall.

And it's curtains for you and me.
We drew them all too soon
That first afternoon
For some privacy.
But does it have to be
Curtains for you and me?

Woke up to hear bulldozers
Rumble through vacant lots,
Saw houseplants we forgot to water
Shrivelled in their pots.
The sun poured through the curtaincracks,
Rained down on you and me —
This column of light,
This dancing dust,
Is the solidest thing we see.

And its curtains for our city —
Where poor people are
The highway and the car
Will get priority.
But does it have to be
Curtains for you and me?

What-I'm-Not Song
(Finale rap)

I'm not your Little Woman
I'm not your Better Half
I'm not your nudge, your snigger
Or your belly laugh.

I'm not Jezebel
And I'm not Delilah
I'm not Mary Magdalen
Or the Virgin Mary either.

Not a Novice or a Nun,
Nor a Hooker or a Stripper,
Not Super Shirley Conran,
Not Jill the Ripper.

No I'm no Scissor-Lady —
I won't snip at your . . . locks.
I'm not a siren, you're not obliged
To get off my rocks.

Not Medusa, not Medea
And, though my tongue may be salty
I'm not the Delphic sybil —
Or Sybil Fawlty

I'm not Poison Ivy
You can throw away the lotion
I'm not your Living Doll
I'm not Poetry In Motion.

And if selling Booze and Cars
Involves my body being used, Well . . .
I'm not Queen Victoria
But I'm not amused.

And if you don't like my Body
You can sodding well lump it —
I'm not a Tart-with-a-Golden-Heart
Or Thinking Man's Crumpet.

I'm not your Woman of Achievement
Not your Slimmer Of The Year
I'm not Princess Diana . . .
No Frog Princes 'Ere!

I'm not little Ms. Middler
I'm not little Miss Muffet
Make me An Offer I Can't Refuse —
And I'll tell you to stuff it!

'Cos I'm not your Little Woman
I'm not your Lady Wife
I'm not your Old Bag
Or the Love of Your Life

No, I'm not your Little Woman
Not your Better Half
I'm not your Nudge, your Snigger
Or your Belly-Laugh!

Team Efforts and Assorted Revues

TICKLY MINCE
(Merryhell Theatre Co., 1982)

THE PIE OF DAMOCLES
(Merryhell Theatre Co., 1983)

A BUNCH OF FIVES
(Wildcat Theatre Co., 1983)

RED HOT SHOES
(with choreographer Peter Royston, the Tron Theatre Club,
Christmas Show, 1983)

SAME DIFFERENCE
(Wildcat Theatre Co., 1984)

Merryhell Theatre Company was: actors; Siobhan Redmond, John Cobb and Kevin McMonagle. Some music was by Esther Allan, and some was by musical director Graham (Mendel) Whitelaw who played piano in both *Tickly Mince* and *The Pie of Damocles*. Writers were Tom Leonard, Alasdair Gray and (he joined us for "The Pie") Jim Kelman and I. Tom's black, black ironies and satires on the Lebanon, the New Right, the Media, West of Scotland sectarianism and chauvinism; Alasdair Gray's insane Grant family, his moneyed braggarts and blusterers, his quick shifts of dramatic power in curt sketches, his deranged respected old politicos; Jim Kelman's surrealist pubs and monologuing gamblers, and grim almost folk tales — like the story of "The Hon" that comes up out of the lavatory pan ("Yi nivir know the minit") meant that the broad rather lightweight stuff I wrote for these revues had plenty of stronger, more solid, meatier material contrasting with it. The performers in their borrowed tartanry had an almost manic energy. I will never forget Kevin McMonagle (Old Blue Eyes) singing Tom Leonard's brilliant version of "My Way" ("though some may mock/the macho talk/upon the Walk/of No Surrender/I've drank the rent/I've clocked the wife/I've spewed my ring upon the fender") or John Cobb as Alasdair's sad flowerseller, or Siobhan

Redmond's Bo'ness hippy.

After seeing *True Confessions* and *Tickly Mince* Dave Anderson and Dave McLennan of Wildcat Theatre Company expressed interest in my working with them. At the end of 1982 I joined the two Daves, Tom Leonard, Sean Hardie, as the fifth writer on the revue *A Bunch of Fives*. (There were five performers too.) It wasn't easy to make a show with such diverse voices pull together and some of what I wrote didn't fit in (I kept it for *The Pie of Damocles* later that year though). But I got to write songs with Dave Anderson and Rab Handleigh for the first time and the reggae "Interference song" which Terry Neason sang was a thrill for me as I'd always wanted to write something for her absolutely amazing voice. "Promises" song was music first (that's hard and I've only done it once since) and "Sincerely Yours" was Rab Handleigh's "tribute" to Barry Manilow which he performed with perfect schmaltz suavity.

Wildcat then gave me a commission for what turned out to be *Same Difference* the following year. This was by far the most enjoyable experience I'd had working in the theatre. It was a musical farce with a classic swap of identity plot with people confessing to their partners their infidelities in the mistaken belief they were confiding in someone else, a daft Midsummer Musical comedy with Gerry Mulgrew as a manic, fast-talking Marlowesque (*Philip* Marlowesque I mean) magical dog who had Puckish powers to cause confusion in his neck of the woods — a hideous fictional Glasgow ghetto housing scheme called Low Cassil. Elaine Smith was very warm and moving as Josie Riley who at thirty-eight with the kids grown is all energy for the community and conceives a very requited fancy for Bazz Blacker, the well-meaning social worker downstairs. Rab Handleigh's Bazz was quite wickedly funny singing "Serial Monogamy" Jack Jones-style, apart from the fact he was wearing Josie's clothes and identity. It *was* a bit everything-but-the-kitchen-sink on sexual politics, and its switches from comedy to Myra McFadden's chilling incest victim's song might have been a bit startling, but I still felt pleased with it and learned (I hope) an awful lot from it, mainly about structure which I find *hard,* and how to pinch plots from people who knew how to do it.

At Festival time 1983, Fania Williams, who had just taken over the Tron in Glasgow, asked me if I was interested in fairy tales. I showed her my book of poems, "The Grimm Sisters", and she asked if I'd like to work with a choreographer on a "dance piece" which would be a grown-up Christmas show with words and music and story, but mainly dance. It was to be about the "wicked stepmother" in Snow White, something from her point of view, redress some of the balance. I didn't know if I could work with a choreographer. What language would we have in common? But Peter Royston, of Scottish Ballet, had a *great* sense of humour and exactly the right touch.

I think "Red Hot Shoes" *nearly* worked. Which was amazing as we started working together far too late, there was a shoestring budget, dancers speaking on stage for the first time. But there was all the experience and help of Ann Scott Jones who somehow managed to make the lonely job of the Usherette/Narrator come to life, and the magic of Hildegarde Bechtler, the designer, turning the Tron into a real 'Forties cinema with help from the hardpressed stage manager, Gibby, and somebody's wonderful collection of cinema architecture bric-a-brac and memorabilia.

Best of all was Peter Royston's eight-minute dance which told all-you-can-remember from Disney's film — it was as if the cartoon had come to life as there she was, on points, bluebird balanced on her finger . . .

I'd love to work with him again.

Not many of the words are worth anything at all by themselves. Included here are a couple of skits on motherhood and a "sound-piece" of nostalgic Glaswegian which played against a 'Forties black and white movie as three dancers with ice-cream trays made moving silhouettes. Multimedia, eh?

Calderpark Zoo Song (from a given line by Tom Leonard)

Wir nocturnals are insomniac
And canny sleep till dark —
A' us animals are crackers,
Here in Calderpark.

Oor dromedary's plenty duende,
Wir porcupine's been in the wars,
Oor zebra's got zero libido —
He kerries aroon
His ain prison baurs.

Aw bit, naw bit, yiv goat the wrang
Orangutang —
Aw bit, naw bit,
Oor orangutang's goat Angst.

The introverted ostrich hates
The manic marmoset
And oor ibex is
A nervous wreck, she's
Constantly under the vet.

Fact is, wir praying mantis
Is a prey to irrational fears,
And big Amanda
The panda
Husnae had it for years.

Aw bit, naw bit, yiv goat the wrang
Orangutang —
Aw bit, naw bit
Oor orangutang's got Angst.

Wir hyena's pure hysterical,
Wir chameleon's two faced
That big laugh
The lanky giraffe
Won't genuflect to the Human Race.

Aw bit, naw bit, yiv goat the wrang
Orangutang —
Aw bit, naw bit
Oor orangutang's goat Angst.

Oh they spike oor buns wi valium
And we swally 'em, we swally 'em.
Me an' the African Sociable Vulture
Urny happy in this alien culture —

Wir nocturnals are insomniac
And canny sleep till dark —
A' us animals are crackers,
Here in Calderpark.

Verena: Anklebiters
(Monologue)

Busy? Busy! Honestly I have been Up To My Eyes in it recently. I mean with Derek you never know whether he's going to get home or not. I mean last week the choppers werny even gettin in to pick them off the Rigs what with the gales and that so *basically* I've just got to expect him when I see him.

Well I thought I'd just do a freezer shop anyway — just the basics basically plus one or two Little Extras, just the odd thing Derek likes, just in case . . . See that Marks and Spencers seafood lasagne Derek could eat that to a band playin . . . Honestly that plus my homemade crême caramel made in the individual ramekins and he's happy as Larry. Practically lies down and *purrs* . . .

Well it's nice to roll out the red carpet, isn't it? So, I'd an appointment in town at the hairdressers and for a legwax and that you don't want to let yourself go I don't want him to get back and catch me with my knickers down and my nail varnish all chipped . . .

Well I was just tidying myself up, och just a week lick of lipstick and a puffa blusher *basically* when I noticed that my mascara was on its last legs so I had to remind myself to stop by at Frazers Innoxa counter as any other tearproof bar theirs brings me out in *lumps*, so to cut a long story short I just nicked in the sidedoor — honest to god I was festooned with carriers laden down like a workhouse donkey — *and* I'd to cut through the shoe department. Well, they'd a sale on in those Italian shoes, you know Thingwiricci — the sort you normally pay an arm and a leg for, well — they're nice aren't they, as the saleslady said herself they are a lovely wee wearing shoe, and very reasonable. So, I was just leaving when I saw them, the five inch heel, crossover ankle strap, glacé kid, suedetrimmed ridiculous! *And* I was just squeezin maself into a five and a half when Moira McVitie round the crescent in the cul de sac comes by and shouts out "Hiya there Verena is that you trying on some fuck-me shoes for yer man gettin back." Excuse me for swearing but I'm just repeating what she said . . .

Well, I did not know wherr to look, shoutin' it out just like that. And in the House of Frazer! Moira McVitie is supposed to be intelligent as well. Always going on about the Fate of the Graduate Wife and how she's fed up being a cabbage — well as far as I'm concerned I cannot see the call for langwidge. I mean I did not need to stay on at school or get my B.A. at Strathclyde to know when not to F or C. Fuck-me shoes, I just handed them back to the saleslady with as much dignity as I could muster and says, thanks but no thanks, I don't know when I'd ever have the occasion to werr them.

Well, I shopped on regardless. The July Sales are a great idea for Christmas shopping particularly in slashed-price discontinued toiletries and I found several nice wee stocking fillers for Derek in the Novelty line and looked in vain for a birthday card for our Joy's eldest but there was nothing suitable. I says have you nothin nicer for a nephew she says "Well if its not there we don't have it".

He's really gorgeous wee Simeon although our Joy lets him schlepp about like a Toerag. Derek and me went along to the new wans Christening and he was like a tink! I goes c'mere to your auntie Verena you're giving wee Evita a showing up, your New Wee Sister, I says your auntie will wipe the gateau off your ear but he jist laughed up his sleeve at me as per usual.

I says to Derek going home I'd prefer a girl wouldn't you. O definitely he goes. If it ever came to the crunch . . . Not that None of a Family's not what we both want what with our lifestyles.

Course I did ask once when I went to the family plannin for a smear. Well, you wonder if all is well. Tubewise and that . . . So I asked them. Wish I'd never bothered. Cue for a questionnaire. Into the ins and outs of everything. Did I always have A Orgasm? I goes of course Derek wouldn't have it any other way. Then it was "Did I always lie still for at least fifteen minutes afterwards?" Cause apparently it can fall out . . . excuse me . . . personally I says I don't leap up, fling back the duvet and shake and vac the shagpile.

The upshot of it all was that *they* wanted *me* to ask Derek would he come in for a sperm count.

Honestly if it was them that had to stuff those navy blue fitted sheets into the automatic after he's been home they'd be Under No Delusions.

Personally, apropos of Wedding presents I often think that the deepdye polyester is not necessarily the best buy for newly weds when you come to think about it.

I'm not one hundred percent sure Derek is really keen. I mean Kids . . . He's a bit of a thingmy Derek. W.C. Fields.

Anklebiters, thats what he calls kids . . . Anyway I'm not sure they're compatible with an offwhite fitted carpet.

Sometimes It's Hard
to be a Woman
(Parody)

Sometimes it's hard to be a woman
Giving all your love to jist wan Man —
You'll have bad times
He'll have good times
Goin' oot on the randan
But if you love him
Bite your tongue and pass another can
And if you love him
Be proud of him
'Cause after all he's Jist a Man.

Stand by your Man
Send oot fur pudding suppers —
When you are on your uppers,
Eat spam yoursel', buy pope's eye
Tae feed your man —
A decent wummin aye hus
Some squerr-slice in her frying pan.
To satisfy her Man.

Sometimes it's hard to be a woman
Stuck in wi' the weans without your Man —
Though he gets pished on peyday
Never mind hen, every Friday
He'll bring you hame a Babycham
If he tends to thump ye
Before he tries to hump ye
Then snores while you lie hatching up a plan
To up and leave the schunner
Oh is it ony wunner
If you can't bloody stand your Man.

Stand by your Man
Give him two arms to cling to
And something warm to come to
When nights are cold and lonely
Stand by your Man
And tell the world you love him
Keep giving all the love you can
Stand by your Man.

The Suitor
(Sketch)

Mrs Grant and her Deirdre's young man. He is perched uncomfortably on a settee with a photo album on his knee. She by his side.

Mrs Grant:	I want you to know, Douglas, that the thing that hurts Mr Grant and I the most is the deceit.
Young Man:	Robert . . .
Mrs Grant:	That's Mr Grant and me with him in his Korea uniform. Its the underhand way you went about the heavy petting and damp carry-on, Douglas.
Young Man:	Mrs Grant, I —
Mrs Grant:	Are you trying to deny you're responsible for her condition? Oh she's always been a good daughter up till now, I'll grant her that, I've never been one to just blame the girl, Douglas, I blame the boy too. A decent girl, until you came along and interfered with her. I'm not a well woman, Douglas.
Young Man:	But I never even —
Mrs Grant:	Half my body has been cut away by the surgeon's knife. Lies, Douglas, if there's one thing I can't thole it's a lie. It's my humble belief you only did it to hurt me, oh yes, spit on the bourgeois, épater the middleclass, oh aye, get your own back on Mr Grant and me for our fitted carpets and crinoline toiletroll covers when you grew up on berr linoleum in a singelenn' in Bridgeton. *(Crying in justified woundedness)* Oh I can just see you lyin' there five year aul' in yer bed recess with your sixteen brothers and sisters eating snotters and planning to trap our Deirdre, tie her down by fair means or foul.
Young Man:	Mrs Grant, my Dad's a chartered accountant. He plays golf, I grew up in Bearsden. Listen Mrs Grant I never even touched your daughter! I wouldny lay her with a bargepole

	— I wouldny touch her with a fingerstall! If she were the last lassie in the world I couldny —
Mrs Grant:	Oh, so you find her *unattractive* do you? Listen, who's been telling you stories? Who's been gossiping to you about her running away with the married man when she was fifteen and ending up in the Daily Record? Did they big mooths next door huv tae clipe about the topless gogo dancing in the Albany? Unattractive? Ah'm worn to a frazzle fighting off the toffs that have been swarming round this door since she was nine and three quarters.
Young Man:	Mrs Grant she is a lovely girl, I don't deny that, but —
Mrs Grant:	Lovely! Lovely! Lovely ma sweet arse, Douglas. Excuse ma French! She takes after *his* side. She's got his hair, god love her, canny dae a damp thing wi' it, pair lamb. He's not a hundred percent, Douglas, never has been, do you take my drift.
Young Man:	I'm not sure, Mrs Grant.
Mrs Grant:	*(Gesturing to photos)* Don't you think I was attractive?
Young Man:	Oh yes, Mrs Grant, lovely photos, very nice, yes, you were . . . very goodlooking when you were young.
Mrs Grant:	How do you mean when I was young, Douglas, I'm not old now, not so old a dog couldn't teach a young pup like you a few new tricks.
Young Man:	Mrs Grant, I'll need to be away or I'll miss my bus.
Mrs Grant:	Oh yes I was just reading in the Cosmopolitan how young men of eighteen and women in their late thirties are sexually compatible. Both at their peak.
Young Man:	Mrs Grant, you're well over your late thirties.
Mrs Grant:	And you're well past eighteen too, Douglas. *(They fall into a clinch.)*

68

Encore for the Arts
(Rap for three)

JEEVES, BERTIE and AUNT HORTENSE discuss TV arts coverage. (Bertie rings, Jeeves comes, aunt Hortense sits and waits.)

Jeeves:	Shall I lay it out in the library, Sir?
Bertie:	The sherry tray?
Jeeves:	That very tray *(pause)* *(cough)*. Might I take the liberty of reminding Sir that Sir's favourite programme's on the air soon?
Bertie:	Vair'soon?
Jeeves:	Indeed Sir. I've err plugged it in the library, Sir, so it'll warm up before it starts.
Bertie:	Splendid! *(Looks puzzled)* Err, what is it Jeeves?
Jeeves:	"Encore for the Arts."
Aunt Hortense:	'Course Bertie's aw-fly keen on Op-Ra — Did you catch much of "The Ring"?
Bertie:	Yes, by Jove, it shattered my sherry glass. Cripes, but that Siegfried could sing! And whatsername with the plaits and the horns on her helmet was absolutely rivetting.
Aunt Hortense:	I'm sure the Great British Public took it right to their hearts!
Jeeves:	Encore for the Arts!
Bertie:	But when it comes to Telly Ballet.
Aunt Hortense:	Did you see Nuryev's Nutcracker? It really was outstanding! Seemed to be sort of permanently suspended in mid-air just-so, flat out without ever landing.
Bertie:	Yet I felt his Coppelia was, in the end essentially ersatz — still, Encore for the Arts!
Bertie:	I say, I say, I say Auntie, the telly certainly does do those classic serials *superbly*, don't it Auntie?

Aunt Hortense:	They certainly do Bertie, they're quite, quite brilliant!
Bertie:	Yes, just fancy. Millions and millions of peounds for a few evoc-ative shots of somebody's home-and-carstle through vaseline and old Jeremy Irons doing his voice-over bit and looking suitably moronic!
Jeeves:	Must say I find the idea of the Plebs watching Brideshead in a single-end quintessentially *ironic*!
All:	ENCORE FOR THE ARTS!
Bertie:	Course that Avant Garde stuff 's enough to make you spew
Aunt Hortense:	Sir Kenneth's "Civilization" was so much more civilized than that so called "Shock of the New".
Jeeves:	Begging your pardon, Sir, but some of those alleged artists that get feted on BBC Two
	could paint no better than a monkey in the zoo.
	If they ask me Sir, they're just trying to make a monkey out of you.
Aunt Hortense:	—And yet they're cult figures at the height of their fame.
Bertie:	That's exactly the sort of Stupid Cult that gives culture a bad name.
Jeeves:	Some of those clowns should get back to Billy Smart's!
Aunt Hortense:	Still, Encore for the Arts.
Aunt Hortense:	What do you think of the South Bank Show?
Bertie:	Frankly . . . not much!
Aunt Hortense:	Yee . . .e . . .es, Melvin's annoyingly adenoidal but he has the Common Touch.
Bertie:	Moore's Marbles!
Aunt Hortense:	Babsy Hepworth's bronzes, everything but the kitchen sink.

Jeeves:	David Hockney, Beryl Cook, Elizabeth Frink!
Bertie:	They're into anything outré —
Aunt Hortense:	Roman Polanski's psyche, the post-modernist novella in a nutshell.
Bertie:	A grand old Dame of the Theatre interviewed about how she got her parts!
All:	ENCORE FOR THE ARTS!

Aunt Hortense:	Course Television Coverage of the Arts is mainly a matter of pearls before swine and horses before carts.
All:	Let's keep it in the possession of us Boring Old Farts — and Encore for the Arts!

Jeeves:	One instinctively knows when something is shite!

71

Mullicking Tyre: The Incomers Take the High Road
(Sketch)

Isabel: Och away in wi ye Inverdarroch, ease yir feet oot o' yir wellingtons and come ben next tae the fire fur a wee dram, it's great tae see ye isn't it, Murdo?

Murdo: It is that, lass.

Inverdarroch: Och, Ah've been dyin' tae get up for a weekend amang yirsels. Its that *hectic* up here amang you Heuchtar Teuchtars.

Murdo: Ah Ken, Ah Ken, we get a good laugh anywey at the antics of the incomers.

Isabel: Oh we do that!

Inverdarroch: Where Ah come frae there's never an incomer. It's that unspoilt it'd drive ye roon the bend. A man wid wait a long while fur a Glesca Keelie at a ceilidh and no mistake.

Isabel: Well, we'd no sooner got wirsels rid of the Forsyth film crew and this new lot moved in next door to us. What are they like, Murdo?

Murdo: Och salt of the earth, lass.

Inverdarroch: Real are they?

Isabel: Och *real*, I canny tell you. He's an architect and she's a bisexual social scientist. Och, first of all they were a wee bit, you know, standoffish.

Murdo: Oh aye, they warmed tae us a treat, wance they saw we didny look down on them.

Inverdarroch: Course its a hail different lifestyle . . .

Isabel: Och aye, aye it is that, Inverdarroch. The way they live it's not wrong jist . . . different. Och Ah shouldny laugh, bit what was that party they had like, Murdo.

Murdo: I mean, they try . . . Asked us over for drinks . . .

Isabel: Meant well!

Murdo: Course they did! Asked us ower fur drinks and when we got there — I mean Ah'd had a bath, splashed on some of the Givenchy for

72

	Gentlemen that Isabel got me for ma Christmas and got into ma designer tracksuit just to be casual like . . .
Isabel:	Course the distinctions were wasted on them, likely thought it was Badedas and Adidas.
Murdo:	So they likely did, lass — but och shouldny laugh —
Isabel:	There she was in the wellies the hameknitted Aran jumper and the stonewash dungarees.
Murdo:	Och its her that wears the dungarees in that hoose right enough.
Isabel:	Well all the better for the breastfeeding — Do you know, Inverdarroch her wee Roderick-dhu, he's four and a half . . .
Inverdarroch:	Roderick-dhu? Roderick-dhu? How do they think them up?
Isabel:	There's Morag . . . and Sommerled, and Seonid and Eachan and Pibroch!
Invergarroch:	Pibroch!
Isabel:	Ah thought oor Damian was gonny burst a gut laughin' when he cam back fae the school and tellt us whit Miss Mackenzie had had tae pit in the register, the day the incomers signed on.
Murdo:	Ah gave him a clip roon the ear and tellt him and Sebastian no tae laugh at poor unfortunate incomers they don't know any better.
Isabel:	Well, wee Roderick-dhu though, he's four and a half and she still breastfeeds him.
Murdo:	*(Blinking)* Constantly!
Isabel:	Its ma rule of thumb that if a wean's auld enough tae ask fur titty then he's too auld tae get but then —
Murdo:	Different strokes for different folks.
Isabel:	Not wrong jist —
Murdo:	Different.
Isabel:	Naw bit there was that Frazer.
Murdo:	Frazer ye cry him, the architect —
Isabel:	Staunin' there in a kilt — an' *(splutters)* a Harris tweed jaikit with dung all ower his

	wellies sayin' name yir poison.
Murdo:	Course I wisnae thinkin so I says Ah'll have a wee cognac and Isabel'll huv a Campari soda!
Isabel:	Ah wished the sanded flerr wid open and swally us.
Murdo:	Course turned oot we had a choice between his homebrew, her cowslip wine or the local single malt.
Inverdarroch:	Nae sophistication, Murdy, nane at a'.
Isabel:	Laugh, Ah thought Ah'd hud a relapse of my cystitis. But listen Inverdarroch, talkin aboot toilet arrangements guess whit they've done.
Inverdarroch:	Whit urr ye gonna be tellin' us noo, Isabel.
Isabel:	They've went and hud an ootside cludgie pit in.
Inverdarroch:	In?
Isabel:	In. In their ootside.
Inverdarroch:	Och away yi go Isabel.
Murdo:	Nae kiddin! Only complete wi tore up squerrs of the Mantchester Guardian. Hung up oan a nail!
Inverdarroch:	Naw!
Murdo:	Aye.
Isabel:	Oot there fur hours tryin' tae strip doon the lavvy seat. *Sand*paper, *paint* stripper. Smell of nitromorse wid off knocked ye ower.
Murdo:	Didny like tae tell them it wis plastic!
Isabel:	We'll make sure ye meet them Inverdarroch, cause och they're priceless, you'll love them. We'll ask them ower, och no for their tea — a hail evenin' wid be a bit of a strain fur them, but for, ye ken —
Murdo:	A wee tequila sunrise, a wee squint at Calum-beag's new blue video.
Isabel:	Aye a wee quiet night — and then they'll likely ask you in Inverdarroch, to theirs . . .
Inverdarroch:	Och man I cin jist see it. Snottery green pottery, hame made bannocks!
Isabel:	Och dinny Inverdarroch that's them tae a T!
Inverdarroch:	*His* typewriter, *her* knittin' machine, Laura Ashley patchwork kit cushion covers, jugs o' weeds on the mantelpiece and the collected

	works of Lillian Beckwith takin' up a hail shelf of the stripped pine kitchen dresser!
Isabel:	Och but my my! Wid ye jist take a keek oot o' that windae and lukk at whit the silly bitch is daein' noo! Milkin' that bliddy goat again, at it fur *'oors* and 'oors yesterday.
Murdo:	Ah havenae seen the auld Billy lukkin sae pleased wi himsel' since he took the rosette at the Edinburgh Royal Agricultural.
Inverdarroch:	Well it lukks as if I'll have tae mind wan thing when Ah meet your incomer pals, Isabel.
Isabel:	And whit's that, Inverdarroch?
Inverdarroch:	Well ₁. . . and A'll have to be mindin' no tae tak a wee tate o' her home made yoghurt.

Country and Western in Kyle

(Parody: chorus to the tune of "You Picked a Fine Time to Leave Me Lucille")

Kevin: In a Bar-room in Bargeddy
That is where I saw my Lady
From her rhinestone razzledazzle I could tell
Gonna break my marriage vow, girl —
Love her all night, and *How*, girl,
Cause my Bumbee Tartan Cowgirl
Was a Honkytonk Bluebell.

Chorus
What is it that satisfies
'Bout cheating ways and lies,
Sad hearts sung sentimental style
Why so much, Country and Western In Kyle.

Siobhan: Well, I looked sorta Hard to Get, son
So he straightened up his Stetson
And he stuck his shrinkfit Levis in his Fryes
Well mibbe I was tipsy
But I heard my twotiming lips say
You're my true bluecollar gipsy
I can see it in your eyes.

Kevin: Well, I'd jist got my Giro,
So I asked her for a Biro —
If she filled in my Pools I might be lucky
But a beggar cayent be a chooser
The working man is a loser
Whether from Beith or Tuscaloos', or
Kilmarnock or Kentucky.

Chorus
All: What is it that satisfies
'Bout cheating-ways and lies
Sad hearts sung sentimental style
Why so much Country and Western in Kyle

Siobhan:	The appeal is international
(talking)	Figger it oot, ah never did,
	The connection between oor Wullie
	And Billy the Kid.

John: Why sing the song of the Clyde, as
Hearts swell with Pride, as
Another Clydebank closedown hits the News
Yes its cheated hearts that swell as
Some Kiltie redneck in his wellies
Sings out loud and proud to tell us
The heuchter cheuchter Blues.

All: And they've cut, cut, cut the future
Between Thatcher the Bloody Butcher
Siobhan: And that Faded Rhinestone Cowboy cross the
Pond
John: I wanted to be mid-Atlantic man
Now I'm going bloody *frantic*, man
In case they're gonna Nuke us
Tae the back of beyond.

Chorus
All: What is it that satisfies
'Bout cheating hearts and lies
Sad hearts sung sentimental style
Why so much Country and Western in Kyle.

Hillhead Election Song
(Rap for three)

The Graduate:
I've got ten Highers and a Ph.d.
Well, it's an erudite constituency!
The house I live in was once very grand
Now it's hardboard partition bedsitterland.
'S not a patch on what it was before
With twentyfour dymoed nametags on each door.

As I trauchle by the B.B.C. or jog to the Yoonie
Avoiding *another* party pamphlet from some Raving Loonie
About cuts, the E.E.C., how the Pope's Beyond the Pale —
I can't get excited about Save The Whale
When down the Clyde Polaris ticks —

No I'm not interested in politics.

Hyndland Lady:
Course it's not everybody can afford
The luggsury of a Private Ward.
You'll not ketch me complaining about my lot
But we've worked-not wanted-not for what we've got.
Oh many's the sacrifice, many's the Spam sangwidge
To avoid the comprehensive and that disgusting langwidge.
Illiteracy 'n' falling standards and what that'll lead to
And as for the so called unemployed, they need to
Get up a bit earlier and try a bit harder
To bring home the bacon for the larder.
No it's not just the workers in Whiteinch —
We wallyclose wallahs are feeling the pinch.
But I believe in Freedom of Choice
The power of my elbow and my Panloaf Voice
And I point-blank refuse to kowtow to a load
Of loudmouth yobs on Dumbarton Road
Social security scroungers up to their tricks —

But I'm not interested in politics.

78

Partick Woman:
Ah've lived here a' ma life, I'm Partick born and bred
But they've the cheek tae cry it Hillhead!
If the Yerds hudnae shut ma Man wid be workin therr still.
And the boy? — he's no worked a day since he left the skill.
But they're staunin' wi' thur clipboards in the pourin' rain,
   The Souls!
"Could Ah possibly answer a question or two fur the Polls?"
I say "Ah'm a lower upper middleclass defector
From the private zone tae the public sector.
Ah'm a Unionist Cathlick Nationalist who *might* vote S.D.P.
Because I take Great Issue to the monarchy.
Ach the Hale Bliddy Loat o' Thum make me sick.

Naw Ah'm no interested in politicks.

But nothing will never get no better until it clicks
That we're *not* not interested in politics.

West End Blues
(Song)

Sunday morning, West End Sunday morning
Wake up high and dry
On my Sunday morning shelf
Sunday mornings I wake up
All wrapped up in myself.

The long lie is over
So get up for goodness sake
Sunday, all over this City
Strange bedfellows wake
Come together again, or turn the other cheek
Nobody knows the score
There's a queue of girls in the dairy buying breakfast
For far more
Than they bargained for.

I got the West End Blues.
Who is losing who?
Who's Using who's
All the West End News.

Sunday morning, West End Sunday morning
Wake up high and dry
On my Sunday morning shelf
Sunday mornings I wake up
All wrapped up in myself.

The long lie is over
Shake yourself for crying out loud.
Have a coffee light up a cigarette
Sit under its cloud
Last night's hide and seekers, Sunday finds out
    are not the game at all.
Saturday's perfect strangers and lovers will
Feel small
And separate after All.

I got the West End Blues.
Who is losing who?
Who's Using who's
All the West End News.

Interference Song

It's TV Newstime —
It's us and them.
Our brave police passively resist
the undemocratic NUM.
Let's wave the flagging Falklands
that was a TV War —
But the screen goes blank
on El Salvador.

It's a TV election
Labour would knock 'em cold
if there weren't something wrong
with the horizontal hold.
The SDP Alliance
is decidedly lukewarm,
and Thatcher talks platitudes
in a snowstorm.

There is some interference
but this is what you get
Do not adjust your attitudes
Do not adjust your set —
The Great British public
is all too bossable —
Normal service will be resumed
as soon as possible.

If it's TV for kids
then you're *white* we presume
and watching with mother
in a Surrey living room?
If it's TV ads
"The Best Thing on the Box"
you can get all these goodies
if you pull up your socks.

It it's TV for women
it's stricly soft soap
and afternoon crochet —
how to cook, how to cope.
If it's TV for men
then it's something to do
with a bat or a ball
or a billiard cue.

There is some interference
but this is what you get
Do not adjust your attitudes
Do not adjust your set —
The Great British public
is all too bossable —
Normal service will be resumed
As soon as possible.

It's a TV minority
being given its fair say
Black is beautiful!
I'm Glad to Be Gay!
For Asians in Britain.
The Gaelic News —
If you watch after midnight
you might just hear our views.

It's TV nostalgia —
Where Are They Now?
Lord Reith in his dinner suit,
Lady Barnett take a bow.
Cut gless ex-cents
'cause they'd standards to set.
Newsreels of the thirties
lest we forget.

There is some interference
but this is what you get,
Do not adjust your attitudes
Do not adjust your set
If the Great British Public
is really this bossable,
Normal service will be resumed
As soon as possible.

Sincerely Yours
(Song with Rab Handleigh)

A song like I'm singing calms the nerves like Valium
Or Mogadon
Chords on solo piano
Lyrics that don't rhyme and go on longer than you expect
    them to
Go on
A saccharine and simple minded song
Ain't nothing wrong
You can la-along
Now the hyperschmaltz and cuckoo waltz
With synthesizer quivers
Sends megashivers up your spine
It does to mine
Now here it comes, the drums

Chorus
Love is a multi-splendoured zing
This is the chorus I falsetto out such things
As baby-baby I will die without your love
Once I was lost but now I'm found
Send in the clowns
Sincerely yours

A song like I'm singing numbs the brain
A sweet cocaine lobotomy
A song like I'm singing hits the charts
Refreshes Parts, in Hyper-Marts,
And posh hotels with five stars, Airport Bars
Company cars from Motherwell to Mars.
Colonel Saunders deep-fry lullaby
Finger lickin' gooey.
Molasses mid-Atlantic sing-along
While Ronnie kills us softly with his song

Chorus
Crisis-Point Flash, Oh it's a gas
A Swan Song for Europe, bee bop a doo wop
Tomahawk Tops S.S. Twenty
Cloud Nine's mushrooming
As Manilow sings sweet an' low
What a way to go
Sincerely Yours

A song like I am singing calms the nerves like Valium
Or Mogadon.
A song like I am singing sweetpea fog, an LA smog like
  cotton wool
between the DJ's ears his smiles 'n' tears will calm your fears
  but that's cool
Now take a breath and hold this note.

Now there's a key change, God knows why
Girl I will love you till I die
Tie a yellow ribbon
Our love's like a red balloon
Fly me to the moon
Till all the seas run dry
Sincerely yours, Sincerely yours.

Promises
(Song)

Puffed up promises
On TV ads
Make you want what you never had

All you Persil Mums
And Flora Dads
Say you live just for the Kids

All you want
is for things to be right
Its Comfort Soft
Its Whiter than white

Buy them Heinz's Beans
Never forget
To buy the fruitgums for Mum's pet

Puffed up promises
Puffed up wheat
Safety, Warmth, Enough to Eat

All you want
Is Life for them all
But who'll be to blame
If the bombs start to fall?

So count the cost of the holocaust
Stand up and fight
For peace.

Apple Pie

When you've a bun in the oven
Everything is apple pie
Men on buses give up seats for you
And don't give you the eye.
A man will tip his hat to you
But never nip your bum.
Even your ma-in-law will grovel
With total approval
At the contents of your tum.
Yes, when you've a bun in the oven
Everything is apple pie.

I'm a lady-in-waiting, I am
Into blatant understating
When you're in the club —
The minute
Its's confirmed that you're in it,
You barber off your locks
And to celebrate your new serenity
You take to wearing smocks.
You indulge
Your non existent bulge
In a pash for Laura Ashley
Who you said you'd never
Be seen dead in ever —

But when you've a bun in the oven
Everything is apple pie
Though first the news you're overdue
Is a bolt from a blue sky
Soon he'll warm to marriage and the chapel,
You're the apple of his eye!
All His, and he knows you're gonna
Make a swell madonna —
No problem, Hushaby!
Cause when you've a bun in the oven,
Everything is apple pie.

A Mother Worries

From the moment the Little White Bundle is stuck in your
    arms
And you're terrified in case you drop it, or it stops breathing,
And, whether it's three hundred decibel howls mean a
    terminal tumour
Or else it's "only teething" . . .
Or else it's the Croup, the Colic, the Beads it just swallowed
    or double pneumoniacutependicitis . . .
(And then when they're older, a mother tends to worry about
what the reason for the Ominous Quiet is)
But let's face it, in this infectious old world
Itching with Lasa Fever, diphtheria, smallpox, meningitis,
    teenage pregnancy, gonorrohea and infantile paralysis.
While all a mother's got is a bottle of Dettol
    in the final analysis.
Well . . . A Mother Worries.

A mother knows she shouldn't try and keep them tied to the
    apron strings because they're bound to flee the coop
And the best a mother can hope for is that they'll occasionally
    pop home for the odd loan of ten quid or bowl of chicken
    soup,
But A Mother Worries.

A mother does her level best to warn them about the ever
    present dangers
Of alcoholism and sex and dope and taking sweets from
    strangers
But it's all water off a duck's back
As well to save your breath
Consideration of a Parent's Wishes
Is a fate worse than death —
Try and instil a sense of what's right
And still they treat this house like a hotel —
Day in day out, morning noon and night.
Well a mother doesn't want to nag or harp on, or use clichés
    or run the risk of sounding shrewish
But a mother whatever her colour and creed is fundamentally
    Jewish —
She worries!

Usherette Scene

NETTIE, SALLY and QUEENIE are usherettes/ice-cream girls with trays.

Queenie: I should of stayed on. Should've stayed on I suppose and got some qualifications. But you never listen, do you, not at that age. Fifteen. Water off a duck's back. Wanted to start living. Wanted excitment. Wanted a paypacket on a Friday night and a new skirt out of C and A's on a Saturday. Wanted life. Big joke, ribbon of dreams, the movies . . . Ended up shining my moonbeam torch on other people's big night out. Went to work in the Regal, some movie palace, a right fleapit. Manager, Mr Rex King . . .

Nettie: Golden Divans Three and Nine, back stalls two and nine, front stalls one and nine. You've missed the beginning of the full supporting feature . . .

Sally: Some night aff. As well stine in. The Majestic. Over twentyfives night. Bunch a bloody geriatrics. "You dancin' " . . .

Nettie: Queenie, stock up with butterkist its verr near the intermission!

Sally: "Naw its jist the wey Ah'm staunin' haw-haw yir patter's like watter." Re-*partee*, that will be right! Tried to get us to stey up fur a slow wan. Nae chance!

Nettie: Hard bith her, seen the Nun's Story twenty seven times and never grett wance . . . you mibbe need merr Mivvis . . .

Sally: Likely merrid onywey.

Nettie: Ah'd dae onythin, tae get oot of this dump . . .

Sally: Gee me a dissy? An' Ah don't think. Who Kerrs? Definately not Deborah! Pure hackit anyhow Ah'd never have lumbered him in the daylight.

Nettie: Night school. Only therrs nae night school durin' the day. An' at night Ah'm workin'.

Sally: Ah goes listen Romeo you been in the Furrin' Legion? Desert disease he hud. Wanderin' Palms . . .

Nettie: Shorthand typost . . .

Sally:	Big Senga got a lovebite affa guy that was the dead spitta Bible John, no kidding ya.
Nettie:	Pitmans. Contometer operator, they get good money . . . Away'n Lysol the lavvys — and Sundays stuck an Irish sixpenny bit in the spray perfume 'hing.
Sally:	Knock knock who's therr, Eureka. Eureka Oxterguff, na hauff, see the Majestic, the smella lacquer in the lavvys wid've knocked you miroc amok never mind knocking back the quarter bottle.
Nettie:	You're ver near outa S.T.s in the ladies, Queenie. Machine's emmty.
Sally:	Want a wee dab of Evening in Paris?
Nettie:	Tell her no, it'll take the colour out of your cardigan!
Sally:	He goes you smell gorgeous is that California Poppy I goes merr like California syrup of Figs sumdy's let aff, definately.
Nettie:	Dampt disgrace that couple that done it in the Golden Divans.
Sally:	*(Shouts)* Drinks on sticks! *(To herself)* Oh don't! Ah was affronted fur her, imagine gettin' stuck 'n' huvin' to get rolled on to a stretcher, the perr o' them, and kerted oot covered up wi' his poplin shortie. *(Shouts)* Tubs!
Nettie:	And you'd huv thought a choc ice wouldny have melted in her mouth the wey she cam' in clutching her quarter of matinee mixture quite the cats pyjamas her fur collar swagger.
Sally:	Butterkist! Kiaora!
Queenie:	Mr King's nice isn't he . . .
Nettie:	Mr King! He's the manager!
Sally:	Sex mechanic! Thon wee Marie Tress that used to work the upper circle got stuck ahint the safe in the office way him an he vernear tane the blouse affer . . .

(Burst of national anthem with them very bored, cracking gum etc., then lights change and they come together to do a little knackered home-time dance, they sing unaccompanied by the silver screen.)

91

All:	You can dance like Ginger Rogers
	You've a figure like Marilyn Monroe
	You've been a blonde since a week last Thursday
	So yir roots haven't started to show . . .

	Yiv a beestung mooth like Joan Crawford
	Yiv got Bette Davis eyes
Nettie:	Yi'd have legs like Betty Grable
	If it wisnae for the varicose thighs.

Sally:	You've been rode merr often than Trigger
	By the light of the silvery moon
	Ye think he's Clark Gable, turns oot he's
	The Creature Fae the Black Lagoon.

All:	Ye can sing like Judy Garland
	Ye can whistle like Lauren Bacall
	Yir lovelier than Liz-beth Taylor
	But still yir worth —
	(Interrupted by the sleazy pinstriped figure of Mr
	King)

Mr King:	Pack it in girls! Queenie, come up to my office right away will you, I want to go over a mistake in the takings.

The Babygrow Song (The Naked Truth)

When naked you fall into the world
(Nothing newer, nothing truer)
You can gurgle in a true and brave new world
Or you can lie and squirm in a sewer.
Depends on whose you are,
Depends on whose you are, and Who's Who
In the pecking order of the Human Zoo.
And that's the naked truth
Yes that's the naked truth.

So grow, baby grow
How you'll end up I don't know
How you'll end up I don't know

Whether ma's on the breadline, or daddy's got loot
(silver spoon or dummy tit)
You will look cute in your birthday suit —
But depends on how you button it.
Depends on what you are,
Depends on what you are, and what's what,
On the sort of naughty bits you've got.
And that's the naked truth
And that's the naked truth.

It's a Dog's Life (Toby's Song)

Toby Dug: I'm a Mad Bad Dug
I'm Toby the Dug
Alsatian tae the oaxters
wi Labrador's lugs
I've Irish Setter's eyebrows
(ain't they set real neat?)
I've got Bulldog's drumsticks
And Saint Bernard's feet.

I'm a dog.
Top dog.

Girls: Dubby Dooh Wah. Dubby Dooh Wah.

Toby Dug: Ma Da wis half boarder-collie
Half Doberman Pinscher —
Ma Maw goes "Help Ma Black Boab!"
When ma da came to winch her
Well, it wis kinuffa a case o'
Lady and the Tramp —
A bit o' a vamp,
A high-class bitch, my ma —
Nine tenths purebred Alsatian
One part je-ne-sais-quoi —

Girls: Dubby Dooh Wah, Dubby Dooh Wah.

Toby Dug: But I'm a dog.
Top dog.
Stare me straight in the teeth
And I'm sure you'll agree
I've got a high class pedigree
I don't gie' a monkey's for the world
and its wife
It's a dog's life!

Girls: Top dawg! Dubby dooh wah, dop
dubby dooh wah, dop, dop, dop.

That's Why the Princess is a Puke

(Sandra's Song)

(Tune: 'The Lady is a Tramp', but becomes punk double time in second verse)

Her herrs always golden, her slippers are glass
Though dumb she'll become some rich man's tits 'n' ass
If she starts out a goosegirl she'll shit on her class
That's why the princess is a puke.

She don't regret Debrett pedigree,
Won't sell herself short and in short she ain't free
When flat on a mattress feels the need of a pea —
That's why the Princess is a puke.

Babe this bint can't love she can't share
Or let doon her hair
This parasite is too uptight
She'll squirm in her ermine, refuse to be shook —
That's why the princess is a puke.

She's had a bobbed nose job, she's lukked doon it since
Hung oan to her cherry jist to merry a Prince
Wi jumbo size ears and a heid full o' mince
That's why the Princess is a puke.
Puke Puke Puke Puke!

A Bit of the Other
(Trish and Frank's Song)

Trish:
I don't know what I see in him
But a bit of the other
He's not exactly the kind of guy
One could take home to mother
But I see myself in a different life
A tied and a true and a tidy wife —
Oh its all for the fantasy, one suspects
One puts up with the sex for the secret,
One puts up with the secret for the sex

Frank:
I know exactly what I see in her
We don't much like each other
She's no a wummin I'd call a wummin
Like ma wife or my mother
But when I turn to her and part her thighs
I pull the wool over Josie's eyes
And I've got something of mines that no one suspects,
I put up with the sex for the secret,
I put up with the secret for the sex.

Frank and Trish:
Lies, Secrets and Silences
Lies, Secrets and Silences
Pull the wool
Cock and bull
The crocodile tear, the Judas Kiss
The snake in the grass with ssseductive hiss
Will sink his fangs in your wedded bliss
Lies, secrets and silence, Lies, secrets, silences!

Change of Life (The Usual)
(Josie's Song)

It's ma thirty ninth year
And the kids are grown
Soon Frank and me will be on our own
Maw and Paw Kettle wi' a colour TV
Thorn Birds, Dallas, Dynasty
The fifty seventh variety
Of sweet damn all
Drives me up the wall
And them next door that don't get along
Are playing our song
They're playing our song
I'll die of boredom if I live that long —

Sitting waiting
Waiting for the change of life

Chorus
And I don't know what I want
But what I want's
Not this
I don't want Frank's kiss
Cause it's jist
The Usual

I see Frank an' me sat there,
I repeat
Till our bums wear through the three piece suite
The Hoover's on the blink but I don't care
Polyester, teflon, tupperware
Gets you nowhere —
Such sweet damn all
Drives you up the wall
If your rent is late the slightest delay
Means hell to pay
there's hell to pay
For a wee refreshment on Giro Day

Sitting waiting
Waiting for the Change of Life

97

Midsummer Night's Dog
(Toby's Song)

I'm a mad bad dog
I'm a Midsummer Dog
And I'll tummle your world right over
And my wildest night's dream
Cowps this hale bleak housing scheme
And rolls it in the Clover

Bow Wow   Bow Wow

The Christians hate the Muslims
I seen it on the News —
The Cathlicks hate the Proddys
And the Arabs hate the Jews

Bow Wow   Bow Wow

The poor hate the rich
And the ugly hate the pretty
White hates black
And the country hates the city

Bow Wow   Bow Wow

Men have hated Women
Since the world began —
The haves hate the havenots —
And Woman hates Man

Bow Wow   Bow Wow

I canny thole intolerance
That's wan thing I detest —
The old hate the young
And East hates West

Bow Wow   Bow Wow

So I'm glad bad dog
To be a midsummer dog
And to roll you in the clover
While this magic moon shall sail
In two shakes of my tail
I'll tummle your sane World over

So no more underdog
I'm a blood and thunder dog
I'm not a sleeping dog and I won't lie!
I'll not say please
And I'll not beg
Sniff your kickers at the vicars
Hump your leg —
I'm not a sleeping dog and I won't lie!
I'll nosh your sausages
And snap at the nippers
I'll shit on your doorstep
And I'll chew your slippers —
I'm not a sleeping dog and I won't lie!

Men have hated Women
Since the world began —
The haves hate the havenots
And Woman hates Man

Bow Wow   Bow Wow

The Sins of the Fathers
(Sandra's Song)

When I was one I ate a bun
When I was two I buckled my shoe
When I was three I hit my knee
When I was four he shut the door
When I was five, when I was five
When I was five . . .

And the sins of the fathers
Will visit the children
Nightly in their beds.
And there's grown-up women
Who're scared little children
Screaming inside their heads.

I've got hair like Shirley Temple
I've a figure like Marilyn Monroe!

Look at me, I'm only three
Sittin' on ma daddy's knee
Who would guess I'm gonny be
His next victim victim victim.
Shoogy-shaggy ower the glen
Daddy's pet and mammy's hen
Mammy's pet and daddy's nen.

And the sins of the fathers
Will visit the children
Nightly in their beds
And there's grown-up mothers
Who are still little children
In the darkness of their heads.

I'm the King of the Castle
You're a durty wee Rascal!

And the sins of the fathers
Will visit the children
Nightly in their heads.
Men lie beside women
Who are terrified children
In the darkness of their beds.

Shocking shocking shocking
A mouse ran up my stocking
The higher up the mountain
The greener grows the grass
The higher up that mousie climbs
The nearer to my —
Ask no questions, tell no lies,
Keep your mouth shut
Catch no flies.

And the sins of the fathers
Will visit the children
Nightly in their beds —
Nelly ate jam, Nelly ate jelly
Nelly left home with a pain in her —
Don't be mistaken, don't be misled
Nelly left home with a pain in her head.
And the sins of the fathers
Will visit the children
Nightly in their beds.

The Life of Mrs Riley
(Josie's Song)

I was eighteen years old in sixty-four
Another three years till the key-of-the-door!
My Mammy said
When I smell Pink Camay I can picture it yet
John and Paul on my Danse 2
Jumbo rollers in my hair and nothing in my head
My Daddy said.

My Da said no one was good enough —
Rockers were mental and Mods were tough
In sixty-four
And I giggled at Problem Page Advice
And I sappled through my nylons and kept myself nice.
Wore panstick wore Mohair I wore angora
In sixty-four.

There was this lawyer bloke who took a notion —
My Auntie said he would go far
Apparently he was articled
And a . . . sorta trainee at the Bar
You often wonder, don't you?
But what's for you won't go by you
You often wonder why you —
But mibbe I should thank ma lucky star.

Because when — I don't know what it was —
In the clinch, his winching made me ill
Couldny put ma finger on it, but I thought it was
The caked-on Clearsil, the cavalry twill
And — in the Beatle-era
He'd lard mair than a smeara
Brylcream on his crowning glory —
Well to cut a long story —

Stood up this Kenneth went on a blind date
Turned out to be Frank, I thought he was great,
I couldn't wait
For the life of Mrs Riley.

For ma Christmas he gave me an H. Samuel locket
Engraved F.R. loves J.D.
Said I'd find somethin' nice in his pocket
—and a packet of three
And for him wel I went for
A lovely charcoal jumper
That I got out Marks and Spencer
And wrapped it round the Hollies new LP

When emdy asked us was it getting serious
We laughed and said we had no future plans
Hogmanay saw Frank and me delirious
On five pernod and blackcurrants plus four cans
Of special plus a snakebite
We didny know how to make right
And we arsed a half bottle of bacardi . . .
At Jessie Pearson's party.

We kissed and we kissed till we couldny resist —
Totally pissed! We were in no fit state —
But I couldn't wait
For the life of Mrs Riley.

We switched Luxemburg up till full volume
And jammed a chair below the handle of the door
It was Jessie Pearson's wee brother Paul's room
There was, I think, another couple on the floor
Frank said everything would be all right
Luxemburg announced A-mami night
And Horace Batchelor's Infradraw —
It didny work at a' —

By Valentine's day I was five weeks late
I couldn't keep doon a thing I ate.
I couldn't wait
For the life of Mrs Riley.

My Mum said I was too easily led
Better call the banns cause we'd made our bed
We'd have to lie . . .
I wore a lemon tent dress down the aisle
When I look at the photys I have to smile —
To say we could have done it different, Frank and I
We'd have to lie!

We've been very happy — nothing great
But I doubt if I would hesitate —
'Cos I couldn't wait
For the life of Mrs Riley.

Bazz's Serial Monogamy Song

We have different lifestyles
The husband-and-wife style's
Not for me.
Me and my Lady live
In Serial Monogamy . . .

A baby carriage
Don't mean a marriage —
That bit of paper is not necessaree
For live-in lovers
What is a love-child or three?
Time the whole world discovers
Serial Monogamy.

Somewhere in between
The teenage libertine
Who nightly paints the town
And the pipe-and-slippers type
Pa-of-Two-Planned-Nippers type
Tied and true and . . . settled down
(All I suspeck —
By heck
Dead from the neck on down) —

There's got to be a Happy Medium
Between till-death-us-do-tedium
The one night stand and cold anonymity
Seems to me —
Could it be
Serial Monogamy?

Nell and Gideon and Sam
All know exactly who I am
(Actually the third Life Partner Trish has had!)
And the older pair call me by my first name too
As if I was (biologically) their Dad!

I've an alternative lifestyle
That husband and wife style
's not for me
Me and my Lady share (more or less)
Serial Monogamy.

Trish's Serial Monogamy Song

Somewhere between
The open marriage
And the bloody rigor-mortgage
The two-car garage
Is ultra sensible
Morally defensible
Home-free, one-two-three
Serial Monogamy.

Would you, should you
Come a cropper
Ten-to-one, old son,
Your "amours" are improper
Peut-etre, I suspect
Politically incorrect
Unlike one-two-three
Serial Monogamy.

Say, mon brave,
You get caught in the lavvy
With thy neighbour's wife
And a bottle of Soave
At how-you-say? — Hogmany
Bugger me, monogamy.
It breaks the monotony . . .

We sing dumb anyway
Turn a blind eye, essentially
And nothing will be said
But don't put a cuckoo in the nest
Or thrush in the un-marriage bed.

Should the Next Man care
To (redeemably) share
My All-My-Worldly-Goods
And be my Old Man, my mucker,
Share my Sartre, my yukka,
My non-sexist breakfast foods,
My Habitat, shabby tat my premenstrual moods . . .

And once it's ended
All is soon mended
No tears, no fears, perhaps three years
And then you part, no?
No broken heart, you're free.
Because no one depended (did they?)
On Serial Monogamy.

For the next in the series —
Or so the theory is —
You're free.
No wedding bells, hell.
Just Serial Monogamy.

Who's Screwing Who —
Who's Paying For All This?

Intro:
Big cities, little lives
Fathers mothers husbands wives
Brothers sisters sons and daughters
Good citizens, good friends —
Can you pardon, make amends?

Verse:
And there's cranes still standing on an empty river,
It's raining and shining on a high-rise tower,
A thousand sordid images
A million middling marriages
Family, community, the nation.
A hardworking past, perilous future —
A hopeless generation.
Here's a tenement that bares a heart we cannot
    comprehend —
Torn wallpaper on a gable end —
One face, a high window.

Chorus:
In the jungle of the cities in this human zoo
Be done by as you're doing to
The fundamental questions show right through:
Who's really screwing who —
Who's paying for all this.

Verse:
Like a world war beginning from a lovers' quarrel
Like a rotten freckle on an apple in a barrel
From the pinpoint of the father's crime
Ripples go out through space and time
Family, communities, nations
And back through the past and into the future
Of unborn generations
And if the marriage bed is an island in a sea of desire
Why oh why do the mothers conspire
With the sins of the fathers.

Intro Form Bridge:
Who screwed up the father
Who screwed up the children
Who are going to screw up theirs
Unless everyone declares
The nuclear family
An A.P.T.

Toby Dug:
Area of priority treatment!

Toby's Verse:
And the show'll go on there's no dress rehearsal
You can drop all the masks, do some role reversal
Learn your part, you've still got time
It's a farce, a pantomime —
All the tricks and transformations
It comes down to the clowning, the pratfalls, the catcalls,
The standing ovations
And if it's a paper moon and just a cardboard sea
We must do more than makebelieve we're free
Or drop the curtain.

Chorus
Will you change yourself, are you going to?
Be done as by you're doing to?
The fundamentals still show through
Who's really screwing who —
Who's paying for all this?

Chorus (Reprise):
In the jungle of the cities, in this human zoo
Be done by as you're doing to
The fundamental questions show right through:
Who's really screwing who —
Who's paying for all this?

New Clichés

Over the past four years, since *True Confessions*, I have been working more on straight drama. *Blood and Ice* (1982) at the Traverse and since rewritten (1984) for a small London fringe company. *Disgusting Objects* for the Scottish Youth Theatre (1982), *Sweet Nothings* for BBC Television (broadcast 1984), *Shanghaied* for Borderline Theatre co. (1983 and revived Mayfest 1984), *Rosaleen's Baby* (1984), Scottish Youth Theatre, and *Dracula* rather freely adapted from Bram Stoker's classic 1897 novel (Royal Lyceum, Edinburgh, 1985).

But between plays and poems odd new characters do begin monologuing away and asking to be written down. Old ones pipe up again on other subjects. Mrs Abernethy grows more awful and Verena is no nearer to what she still can't seem to own up to as her heart's desire. . . . This then is a ragbag of pieces, some still to be performed out loud, which I haven't collected together till now.

I Wouldn't Thank You for a Valentine
(Rap)

I wouldn't thank you for a Valentine.
I won't wake up early wondering if the postman's been.
Should 10 red-padded satin hearts arrive with a sticky sickly saccharine
Sentiments in very vulgar verses I wouldn't wonder if you meant them.
Two dozen anonymous Interflora roses?
I'd not bother to swither over who sent them!
I wouldn't thank you for a Valentine.

Scrawl SWALK across the envelope
I'd just say "Same Auld Story
I canny be bothered deciphering it —
I'm up to here with Amore!
The whole Valentine's Day Thing is trivial and commercial,
A cue for unleasing cliches and candyheart motifs to which I personally am not partial."
Take more than singing Telegrams, or pints of Chanel Five, or sweets,
To get me ordering oysters or ironing my black satin sheets.
I wouldn't thank you for a Valentine.

If you sent me a solitaire and promises solemn,
Took out an ad in the Guardian Personal Column
Saying something very soppy such as "Who Loves Ya, Poo?
I'll tell you, I do, Fozzy Bear, that's who!"
You'd entirely fail to charm me, in fact I'd detest it
I wouldn't be eighteen again for anything, I'm glad I'm past it.
I wouldn't thank you for a Valentine.

If you sent me a single orchid, or a pair of Janet Reger's in a
    heartshaped box and declared your Love Eternal
I'd say I'd not be caught dead in them they were politically
    suspect and I'd rather something thermal.
If you hired a plane and blazed our love in a banner across the
    skies;
If you bought me something flimsy in a flatteringly wrong size;
If you sent me a postcard with three Xs and told me how you
    felt
I wouldn't thank you, I'd melt.

St Valentine's Day Heart Catalogue
(Rap)

1. hearts are always red and shiny
2. hearts come in all colours
3. hearts are made of padded satin
4. hearts can be candystriped
5. hearts make neat pincushions
6. hearts take long slow cooking but with care and the right sauce they rival liver braincheese or sweetbreads any day.
7. Heartbroken Doctor Tells Court How Gorilla Played Cupid (Globe and Mail)
8. 'Ave a 'eart 'Arry she panted and 'ang on a tick! (Cockney porn-novel)
9. King's Road's Mary Quant told the conference that with the advent of the miniskirt in the sixties the crotch had been redefined as the new erogenous zone. Ms. Quant confided to delegates that she often jollied Plunkett (her husband, entrepreneur Alexander Plunkett-Green) into helping her dye her pubic hair some fantasy shade, or to trim it to a neat heart shape. (New Statesman.)
10. Hearts will definitely not be worn on sleeves this season (Harpers)
11. My Husband Had A Heart Transplant And Now He Loves The Donor's Wife (Confession Magazine)
12. The Heart is just another pumping muscle (Doctor Christian Barnard)
13. Having asked for directions from a friendly policeman, here she was en route to his heart, via his stomach. With a half-shudder, she left the lower bowel and set off gingerly along the rather treacherous surface of the greater intestine which coiled before her — a tunnel she wasn't too sure she saw the light at the end of. She wondered if she would have let herself get involved had she known in advance that it entailed so much messing with entrails. However, it was too late to think of that now. She loved him. She was in it, up to here.
14. Heartbreak Hotel offers cheap, out of season rates for Winterbreak Weekends.

15. Heartsease makes a sweet Victorian posy. Combined in a nosegay with love-that-lies-bleeding and a sprig of maidenhair fern, spring brides should find it a piquant bouquet.
16. Heartshaped pastrycutters can make candykisses of common or garden cookiemix. When cool, sprinkle with a little cinnamon and powdered rhinohorn.
17. How the heartshaped sunglasses and the lollipop of Lolita catapulted lovely Sue Lyons to stardom.
18. There are all manner of betrothals, and any are blessed as long as the heart be true.
19. Nowt up with the ticker, any trouble with the waterworks?
20. The heart is a lonely hunter.
21. My heart's in the Highlands.
22. Half a heart is better than no.
23. Remember, don't take any wooden Hearts.

How Do I Love Thee, Let Me Count The . . .

(Rap)

I go ape
I go bananas
I go spare
I go for you in a big way
I go for you with a knife.

I go curly
I get jealous
I act reasonable
I change my mind.

I put on an accent
I slip into something more comfortable
I turn nasty.

I am one man's meat
I am nobody's fool
I refuse to make fish of the one and flesh of the other
I sing dumb
I sit pretty
I stand for my rights.

I am hard hearted
I am self centred
I must be soft.

I play by ear
I use my loaf
I suspect fair play.

I cash in on my sex appeal
I take all the credit
I give you the benefit of the doubt.

I take it as it comes
I take it for what it is
I take it with a pinch of salt
I take it very seriously indeed
I will cross that bridge.

I made the whole thing up from the start to finish
I will make it up to you somehow
I have made you up a bed in the spare room
I have made up my mind.

I am not like that
I am neither here nor there
I am not the same
I am not kidding.

Adultery Song

Chorus
I'm nothing
To write home about
I'm the best thing in your life
But I'm best kept secret
From the kids and the wife

We keep each other's counsel
Find our confidences sweet,
Ignore each other in crowded rooms
Where even our eyes can't meet. —
Till sick of feeling lovesick
We seek temporary cures —
Always my place
Never yours.

Chorus
Because I'm nothing
To write home about
(I'm the best thing in your life)
But I'm best kept secret
From the kids and the wife

We talk of somewheres we'll go sometime
As soon as you can —
Till then I'm snatching stolen time
With a borrowed man.
We salt our suppers with secrecy,
Steal kisses in the park
Then you love me half the night with the light on —
But you keep her in the dark.

Chorus
No, I'm nothing
To write home about
I'm the best thing in your life
But you have to keep me secret
From the kids and the wife.

118

You say you're sorry to leave me
I say it is OK.
And skin to skin we cling once more —
Then you shower love away,
Take the carkeys by my ticking clock,
Go and leave me in my bed
With her photo in your wallet —
My phone number in your head

Chorus
Cause there's nothing
I could phone your home about —
There's the kids, and the wife
Even for a matter of life and death
I can't interrupt your life

Chorus
No, I'm nothing
To write home about
I'm the best thing in your life
But I'm best kept secret
From the kids and the wife.

Bluejohn Pockets

You came to the city.
You came to see me,
Bringing me driftwood you found by the sea.
One night in my tower
And the next thing I knew
I was out on the motorway
Hitching with you
Next to nothing in our pockets
To live on.

It wasn't so always.
Not you and me.
And once this mountain lay under the sea.
Look close at the surface,
You can easily tell
How it changed, how it hardened
To fossilised shell
That lies in deep caves by the pockets
Of bluejohn.

Bluejohn, oh bluejohn
Marbled and scarred
Blue, bright and hard
Oh it runs like a vein through the rock seam.
Never a day but you think of her
And I of him.

It's easy together,
But we need to be free.
You can't cut through rock seams that easily.
Though we went at it goodstyle,
With your penknife,
My nailfile.
And filled up our pockets
With bluejohn.

Bluejohn, oh bluejohn
Marbled and scarred
Blue, bright and hard
It runs like a vein through the rock seam.
Never a day but you think of her
And I of him.

Back now in the city. What can I save
But this mantelpiece full of the bluejohn you gave
Yes we each loved another
But times have moved on
Ask me once to go with you
I'll be packed up and gone
With nothing in my pockets
But bluejohn.

Plenty
(Rap)

Come.
Come and take potluck
eat humble pie whatever.
Midweek I don't promise much
but it'll certainly stretch to one extra, anytime. Plenty.
I've never been one to rustle up
some loaves-and-fishes miracle
out of a mini-tin of storecupboard pomodoro
and a lump of rat-trap cheddar.
God! Our house when we were wee
day-before-payday pan-haggis
was neither here nor there
so I well mind the time
high tea was a glittering vision of a teetering cakestand
and our snottery noses at the pane
well and truly up against it!
Not at all. No. No. Come as you are. Just bring yourself.
Well.
Well if
you're passing one
bottla pink plonk whatever.
Wouldn't go amiss.

Favourite Shade
(Rap)

She's getting No More Black, her.
You've got bugger all bar black, Barbra.
Black's dead drab an' all.
Ah'd never have been seen
deid in it, your age tae!
Dreich. As a shade it's draining.
Better aff
somethin tae pit a bit a colour in her cheeks, eh no?

Black. Hale wardrobe fulla black claes.
Jist hingin' therr half the time, emmty.
On the hangers, hingin.
Plus by the way a gloryhole
Chockablock with bermuda shorts, the lot.
Yella kimono, ah don't know
whit all.
Tropical prints.
Polyester everything Easy-Kerr. Bit naw, naw
that was last year, noo
she's no one to give
nothing coloured
houseroom. Black. Black.
Ah'm fed up tae the back teeth lukkin' ett her.
Feyther says the same.

Who's peyin' fur it onlywey?
Wance yir workin' weer whit yi like.
No as if yiv nothin' tae pit oan yir back.
Black!
As well oot the world as oot the fashion.

Seen a wee skirt in Miss Selfridge.
Sort of dove, it was lovely.
Would she weer it, but?
Goes: see if it was black
If it was black
it'd be brilliant.

Donkey
(Monologue)

I didn't want the donkey. I didn't know whether to go for the oatmeal for second choice or whether to stick to the saxe, but I definitely did not want jet or donkey, that I did know. Mibbe I should send it back.

I never ticked it, it does damn all for me, I don't see why I shouldn't insist on my first colour-choice or nothing.

It was the very same story the time oor Isa sent for the stilettos very much against my advice as it happens but they were supposed to be real made-in-England leather uppers available in three colourways, aubergine, aqua or avacado well, as she said herself she was expecting green but nothing quite as Irish as they turned out in fact to be. She had thought they'd be more of a bottle. What I really wanted was the nigger, or mibbe the navy. I've got sweet fanny adams to go with donkey! A catalogue can mean a pig in a poke, I really don't advise it.

Mrs Rintoul: Standard English
(Monologue)

I'm terrified to tackle poetry with them.

Exactly, Eileen, don't tell me, if they're anything like my 4×4 they'll have you demented . . .

I mean you get Sweet Fanny Adams done with them on the run up to Christmas anyway, E.I.S. Industrial or no E.I.S. Industrial Action and we're only three days back in January before the Prelims, so as far as I can see that is St Agnes's Eve out the window.

So I've just advised them to stick to Billy Liar and a character-sketch and told them to hedge their bets a question will Come Up. As it very likely will.

Turns out they've done damn-all since Flannan Isle in the First Year.

But you give up. I despair. I goes, "4×4, C'mon you've all read the book — read it, it's coming out their *ears* — I goes, let's examine the character of the Witch. You know, his girlfriend, c'mon how would you describe her personality. Give me some words. Not necessarily adjectives. Just words." Course, Derek Weintraub just sat there, totally gormless and I-know-it-all at the same time as only a fifth-year O-level repeat can be. Eventually, after knocking my pan in, and doing my nut generally till I was blue in the face I manage to get a Response out of Annemarie Barr. Sticks her hand up and goes, "Moany." I goes "Annemarie I hope and trust and pray you are not going to put that down on the paper. Could you not at least say 'short-tempered'? Something Standard English anyway . . ."

Made them ink-exercise it for the Thursday and when I got in the results I was tearing my hair. Annemarie's every-second Billy was with a small "b". I goes Annemarie I doubt if there would be any chance for you even under Munn and Dunning unless you can conquer the capital letter.

Actually I am still in two minds about mibbe squeezing in a quick Hughes or a Heaney somehow. I cannot believe that it can be right that this late in the game Poetry is still a closed book.

Mrs Abernethy: Festive Fayre
(Monologue)

Well . . . *wait* till I tell you. It was no Christmas for me this Christmas. Telling you Christmas dinner's no picnic for The Lady of the House at the best of times and this year was no exception. I just said to my hubby this morning, I said, "The sooner its the Sixth of January and we've got a they decorations back up the loft and poked all they clogged-up pine needles out the Hoover tube with a Knitting needle and its back to auld claes and parritch the better pleased I'll be."

Honestly its been bake, bake, bake. The beaters of my Kenwood have seldom been still since the end of November. Between the Cubs Christmas Fayre and the Girls Guildry conversazzione, and I'd two dozen melting moments for the Brownies Bring And Buy. Still it was appreciated and thats the main thing. Brown Owl said to me your melting moments go like snow aff a dyke. Still it'll be with folk knowing where they came from. Our Gillian got terrible food poisoning off strange tablet at a Garden Fete once.

Och but don't mention our Gillian to me. Its her that I'm vexed at. That girl ruined Christmas for the whole family. Well, its a busy time for her dad as well, what with those extra services — and a lamentable feature of this day and age is the amount of toerags that roll in bold as brass to the Watchnight Service *reeking* of drink.

Well, Gillian's always been very independent. Well we've *encouraged* that. We've encouraged that. My Better Half's always maintained, and I agree with him, if they don't want to go to the Church then we won't force them. After all one of the dogmas of the Protestant faith has always been a freedom of choice. I mean John Knox and Martin Luther Thingmy, I mean they built the Kirk on the tenets of independence. I mean I'm no historian, you'd have to check up on this with my hubby, but as far as I know the Reformation started up North in Europe a guid lang mile away from Rome and the Pope and that, up in the Region of what we now know as Holland, and Germany and Alsace Lorraine. In fact, correct me if I'm wrong, but I think that Protestantism was originally an Alsatian Dogma.

So they've not been regular attenders since the age of fourteen or so and their dad and me have always been very tolerant. And Valerie, that the elder girl, has been a model daughter in every other way. Five Highers, Jordanhill, married in the University Chapel to an awful nice electrical engineer who wouldn't say boo, taught for two years till she got her parchment before starting a family. And wee Kate and Joshua are just plain gorgeous even though it's their Granny talking. Valerie's got some wee "do" on tonight and I popped over to Hyndland Road this morning because she was short of ramekins for her starters and the wee souls were all over Gran with their Selection Boxes, honestly any more would sicken me.

But that Gillian . . . Well, she phones me up to say could she bring a friend home for Christmas. I says you know your friends are always welcome, you don't have to ask. So she says Michael and I will be off the six fifteen at Central on the twenty third. Michael. Well, I thought nothing of it, because she's always palled up with a lot of English chaps since she was up at St Andrews and there was the odd Michael among them. Simon and Timothy and what not. Dampt few Alastairs and Kenneths anyway!

So, to cut a long story short, she arrives with this . . . Michael. And he seems very nice. Turns out his Dad is a head master in the Bathgate area so I says "Oh what's the school called?" All innocence. St Francis Xavier says he without turning a hair. I didn't know where to look, and that bisum just sat there cool as a cucumber wolfing down my Celebration Chile Con Carne Surprise. I mean, as I said to my hubby later on, we didn't scrimp and scrape to send her to Hutchy Girls so she would grow up to give us grandweans saying merr, flerr and sterr.

Still, it's her life to ruin and one word from us and she'll do the opposite so good luck to her, I wash my hands, I wash my hands absolutely.

And now there's the Ne'erday to get by. I'll better away and get my black bun out the oven. I don't like to blow my own trumpet but My Better Half could eat it to a band playing. I like it, I *like* it alright, but does it like me, that's the trouble! At least I've my shortbread baked, I wouldn't give the bought stuff houseroom. Willie Learmouth the session clerk came by today for the Intimations and he's an awful nice man, one of Nature's Gentlemen, went to Allan Glen's when that *meant* something, his wife's got a plastic hip but you never hear him complain, anyway he sat down to a wee cup of tea and naturally he could not resist my all butter shortbread "Nettie," says he, "your petticoat tails would melt in a man's mouth."

Mibbe another batch wouldn't go wrong? Happy New Year everybody, although it'll be no holiday for me.

Verena: Castaways
(Monologue)

I've never been a big knitter. Unlike my mother. Never not knitting something. Tension, that's the trouble, she's a terrible slack knitter. Anything she does you tends to damp near drown you. She's good hearted, but basically it's a waste of money for the wool.

Neither oor Joy nor me have ever been handy. Hopeless with our hands. As Joy herself says, I can cast on, I can cast on OK but I canny cast off.

Never been much of a book fan either. Well not till Derek went away Up There. Now I tend to find I need something else to put me to sleep. No, not at all, I'm not nervous, no I've never been bothered with things that go bang in the night. Unlike some. Derek was telling us about some roustabout's wife who *will* flit back in with her mother every fortnight. Back and forth. Terrified. Lovely bungalow in Bishopbriggs an' all. Apparently some of them nervous wrecks. Alsatians and everything. Lodgers. Getting the weans in to sleep with them in the Kingsize and of course will they move back to their bunkbeds once He's back? Causes problems.

Well, I read a lot these days. Well it's either that or TV and that is a lot of damp nonsense as per usual. Not worth the licence fee as Derek says. Of course I am addicted to Alexis although I admit the entire thing is very far fetched. But some of her rigouts are gorgeous and I wouldn't mind getting to that age with a figure like that.

Actually I have been something of a clothesaholic recently, don't tell Derek, but I have to put that fitted wardrobe under lock and key when he's back and hope he doesn't keek in through the louvres because I wouldn't want him to think I was extravagant.

But he likes me to look nice when we go out anyway which is not often, granted. Well as he says when he's at home he likes to get down the pub with the boys for a pint because of course it is dry Up There. Although apparently some of them go to all lengths, resealing Coke cans what have you, to smuggle drink in. Instant dismissal if they're caught as well.

I don't anyway, wouldn't care if I never so much as sniffed it again. Drink's never been either here or there for me, bar a wee Baileys with my coffee if we go out for a meal and I always buy it in at Christmas, because most women like it. Bacardi and coke is my only tipple and I do sometimes get through a couple on nights when I'm in myself, well it's better than turning to the biscuit barrel isn't it? Moira McVitie is fairly putting on the beef since she gave up the teaching when wee Scott was born.

Moira never knows what to be at. Well, as I said to her boredom is all in the mind, it's up to yourself isn't it? Wants to start a Book Group or some damp thing, lending out and discussion groups on a Wednesday morning over coffee. Not my cup of tea. As I said to her we've got two shelves of hardbacks in the alcove because I do think they furnish a room as the man said, but I wouldn't be on for lending them out because you don't know the condition they'd come back in. Sticky fingers etcetera. Some people let their under-fives run riot. But Moira says no it's paperbacks only, insisted on lending us some of those Virgo Books and Woman's Press and that, you know "I Stand Here Ironing" and so on, couldn't be bothered to try and make sense of them. Not what I'd call escapism anyway.

Course I do get the Woman and the Woman's Own plus I swap Options for the Cosmopolitan off our Joy. I wouldn't give Woman's Realm houseroom. Course it's Princess Di and the Queen Mother this that and the next thing.

Actually I am sorry for her. Prince William, Prince Harry, they're only interested in her as a breeding machine. I thought it was a sin publishing her gynaecological details all over the Sun and the Record etcetera before the Royal Wedding.

I mean it's everybody's Own Business as I keep telling my mother and our Joy.

Moira McVitie says she's got a pal that went to that Steptoe's Clinic. I have to laugh, I can't not picture that old, what do you call him, Wilfrid Brambell wasn't it, mind the time he lost his false teeth in the bath and Harold goes 'oh you dirty old man' . . .? Anyway apparently that clinic, you know, they do that, you know, in vitrio fertilisation, test tube babies etcetera. I don't know what all. Apparently they blast you with hormones, so Moira's pal says, to make you ovulate and everybody is sitting around going, "how many eggs did they get out of you? Only six? I produced twelve!" and then of course hubby's got to do the business on them and once they're fertilised they re-implant them, maximum six and

130

hope one of them takes. I cannot picture Derek being up for it quite honestly, can you? I'm not one hundred percent keen on meddling with nature, anyway. It's like all that surrogate stuff. Too commercialised, same as Christmas.

Course Moira always has had a vivid imagination, you have to take what she says with a pinch of salt. Honestly I was round there for a coffee the other day — actually wee Scott was awful quiet. Moira shouts "Scottie is that you up there watching a mummy's and daddy's video?" I had to laugh. Imagine Malcolm, the big intellectual, with a dirty video. And him always bumming on to Derek about how he'd taped the whole of Brideshead Revisited. Who was he trying to impress?

But Moira, you never know what she'll be telling you next. She says there's a Coven round the cul-de-sac. I ask you. I said to her what the hell would anybody be getting involved in all that damp nonsense for? She says boredom. Boredom. Some folk just don't know what to be at.

Postcard Us When the Wean Says Bananas
(The Greeting Card Song)

Happy Silver Anniversary,
Deepest Sympathy On Your Pregnancy,
Birthday Greetings (Humorous),
Please Say Its Not Too Late For Us —
Forget Me Not, Let's Tie The Knot, Thanks a Lot
Gift Much Appreciated,
To a Mother Dear . . ., A Guid New Year, Wish You Were
    Here,
Valentine's Day (Belated).

Was Sad to Hear, So Glad to Hear, Too Bad to hear
Your News.
Someone somewhere wants a card from you.
Drop us a line to say you're fine
And how highly you regard us —
And postcard us
When the wean says bananas.

New Wave Designs, Old Valentines
Or Repro Victorianas
Drop us a line to say you're fine
And how highly you regard us —
Oh, and postcard us
When the wean says bananas.

The Key of the Door, Have a great Yom Kippur,
White Heather for good Luck,
A Hallmark Card, Tell Vernon Ward
Go take a Flying Duck.
Kitten-In-Boot, or Snoopy Cute, or Beryl Cook —
Something Sweet and Silly,
A Billet-doux, A Seaside view or a Bamforth Blue
(I've lost My little Willy).

U.R.21, So It's a Son!, Have lots of fun,
I'm blue!
Someone, somewhere wants a card from you.
Drop us a line to say you're fine
And how highly you regard us
And postcard us
When the wean says bananas.

Roman Orgies, Royal Corgis
or Charleses-and-Dianas.
Drop us a line to say you're fine
And how highly you regard us
And postcard us
When the wean says bananas.

Seasons Greetings, Aw the Best
Good Luck on Your Driving Test
Blank for Your Message, Glad to Be Gay
Have a swell St Swithin's Day,
How you doin'? I love you, 'n' Get Well Soon.
Bon Voyage of course
Please be Mine, Hello Sunshine, the food is fine
Congrats on your Divorce.

I hope you're free, R.S.V.P. With love from me,
To you.
Someone somewhere wants a card from you.
Drop us a line to say you're fine
And how highly you regard us
And postcard us
When the wean says bananas.

Men Talk

(Rap)

Women
Rabbit rabbit rabbit women
Tattle and titter
Women prattle
Women waffle and witter

Men Talk. Men Talk.

Women into Girl Talk
About Women's Trouble
Trivia 'n' Small Talk
They yap and they babble

Men Talk. Men Talk.

Women gossip Women giggle
Women niggle-niggle-niggle
Men Talk.

Women yatter
Women chatter
Women chew the fat, women spill the beans
Women aint been takin'
The oh-so Good Advice in them
Women's Magazines.

A Man Likes A Good Listener.

Oh yeah
I like A Woman
Who likes me enough
Not to nitpick
Not to nag and
Not to interrupt 'cause I call that treason
A woman with the Good Grace
To be struck dumb
By me Sweet Reason. Yes —

A Man Likes a Good Listener

134

A Real
Man
Likes a Real Good Listener

Women yap yap yap
Verbal Diarrhoea is a Female Disease
Woman she spread she rumours round she
Like Philadelphia Cream Cheese.

Oh
Bossy Women Gossip
Girlish Women Giggle
Women natter, women nag
Women niggle niggle niggle

Men Talk.

Men
Think First, Speak Later
Men Talk.